BRIGHT NOTES

THE TURN OF THE SCREW AND DAISY MILLER BY HENRY JAMES

Intelligent Education

Nashville, Tennessee

BRIGHT NOTES: The Turn of the Screw and Daisy Miller
www.BrightNotes.com

No part of this publication may be used or reproduced in any manner whatsoever without written permission, except in the case of brief quotations in critical articles and reviews. For permissions, contact Influence Publishers http://www.influencepublishers.com.

ISBN: 978-1-645421-98-6 (Paperback)
ISBN: 978-1-645421-99-3 (eBook)

Published in accordance with the U.S. Copyright Office Orphan Works and Mass Digitization report of the register of copyrights, June 2015.

Originally published by Monarch Press.
Vartkis Kinoian, 1965
2020 Edition published by Influence Publishers.

Interior design by Lapiz Digital Services. Cover Design by Thinkpen Designs.

Printed in the United States of America.

Library of Congress Cataloging-in-Publication Data forthcoming.
Names: Intelligent Education
Title: BRIGHT NOTES: The Turn of the Screw and Daisy Miller
Subject: STU004000 STUDY AIDS / Book Notes

CONTENTS

1) Introduction to Henry James — 1
2) Introduction to The Turn of the Screw — 11
3) Textual Analysis
   - Introductory Chapter — 16
   - Chapter I — 20
   - Chapter II — 23
   - Chapter III — 26
   - Chapter IV — 28
   - Chapter V — 30
   - Chapter VI — 33
   - Chapter VII — 36
   - Chapter VIII — 38
   - Chapter IX — 40
   - Chapter X — 42
   - Chapter XI — 44
   - Chapter XII — 46
   - Chapter XIII — 47
   - Chapter XIV — 49
   - Chapter XV — 51
   - Chapter XVI — 53
   - Chapter XVII — 55

	Chapter XVIII	57
	Chapter XIX	59
	Chapter XX	61
	Chapter XXI	63
	Chapter XXII	66
	Chapter XXIII	68
	Chapter XXIV	69

4) Character Analyses — 72

5) Critical Commentary — 83

6) Essay Questions and Answers — 91

7) Introduction to Daisy Miller — 96

8) Textual Analysis
   - Part I — 102
   - Part II — 113

9) Character Analyses — 125

10) Critical Commentary — 130

11) Essay Questions and Answers — 135

12) Selected Bibliography and Guide to Research — 140

INTRODUCTION TO HENRY JAMES

LIFE (1843 - 1916)

Henry James is probably the outstanding American novelist and stylist. If he is not alone in that rank, he is accompanied by only three or four others, such as Hawthorne, Melville, Twain, and perhaps Faulkner. Even among those, who represent the best in American literature so far as novelists are concerned, James does seem to stand out if only on the basis of his prodigious lifetime of writing. James's writing career extended from the late 1860s to the first two decades of the present century, and he was without question the first American novelist to truly bring his work into the mainstream of world literature. This is not to say that there were not great works in American literature before James's major novels, but it is to say that James made the American novel something more than the product of an American. He made it an art form, a work as sophisticated as the well-written poem, and his works rank with the outstanding writers not only of America, but also of Europe.

The facts of James's life are best seen in relation to his work, for James lived a quiet life and devoted himself to literature as a profession and as a way of life. The following is a brief summary of some of the important dates, but the next section ("Periods in James's fiction") views James's works as the primary material for understanding him. The student should know at least the following: Henry James was born on April 15, 1843, in a house on Washington Square in New York City. James in his autobiography later told of the impressions he had of life because of the humanity he would observe in that respectable section of the great city. Henry's father, Henry James, Senior, was a well-known figure in intellectual circles. He had inherited his wealth and spent much of his time in cultured activity. The novelist's older brother, William, became famous as a philosopher, psychologist, and professor at Harvard University, and the brothers remained close, as their correspondence shows, throughout their lifetimes. Henry James, Senior, believed that his children should be exposed to the culture and life of Europe as a basic part of their life, so he took his sons there when Henry was still an infant. On their return from their first trip, they lived in New York again, but also stayed in Albany. In 1855 they returned to Europe again for three more years of education, some in school, some at the direction of tutors, and some led by the father, in Geneva, London, and Paris. During 1858-1859 the family stayed in Newport, Rhode Island, a very fashionable resort at that time, where Henry and William studied painting with John LaFarge, a well-known artist. In 1859-1860, however, they were in Europe again, this time in Geneva and also Bonn, Germany. In 1862, James entered the Law School at Harvard, while William entered the scientific school at the same university. In that same year, Henry sustained some mysterious injury to his back that kept him out of the Civil War. Around 1865 James began publishing his sketches, critical reviews, and stories, in such magazines as the famous *Atlantic Monthly* and the *North American Review*. It was just a year before this time that the young Henry James had decided on writing as his profession. The student should understand that James's decision was not an idealistic, romantic outburst, but a reasoned and mature commitment to writing as a career. In 1869 James went to Europe, and although he returned to America on several occasions, one can say that from that year on James was a resident of the European continent. Most students of American literature see James's expatriation as a pilgrimage in reverse of the normal pattern; it was a move, one must understand, made by an artist in order to give himself the proper perspective from which he could continue with his craft. James lived for the most part in London, but he spent some time in Paris, Rome, and other European cities. In 1915, although he was unmistakably an American in thought and art, James became a British subject in protest of American neutrality during that time of the First World War. James died in February, 1916.

PERIODS IN JAMES'S FICTION

Much more complete a view of James as a writer comes from looking at the stages in his long and fruitful writing career. F. W. Dupee in *Henry James* breaks that career into the following periods:

1. 1870s: This is James's idealistic phase. He is learning his craft and developing his themes. The works are really not complicated and characters are clearly drawn without too much ambiguity or complexity. Still James achieved in this early period some of his most memorable characters, such as Christopher Newman in *The American* (1877) and Isabel Archer in *The Portrait of a Lady* (1881). Other important early works are *Daisy Miller*, 1879; *The Europeans*, 1878; and *Washington Square*, 1881.

2. 1880s: James in this period became more realistic. He began to deal with more complicated matters such as

social institutions and political issues. Some important works are *The Princess Casamassima*, 1885; *The Bostonians*, 1886; and *The Tragic Muse*, 1887.

3. Late 1880s and Early 1890s: At this point, James turned to writing for the theatre with noticeably bad luck. He was humiliated on the night of the opening of his play *Gum Domville*, when the audience was vile to him. An interesting note is that a young critic, George Bernard Shaw, was at that performance.

4. 1890s: During this time James started tackling the problem of evil-evil in the sense of strong characters and their relationship to innocent victims. It was during this period, because James was constantly experimenting in the desire to develop his technique, that the reputation of James as a difficult writer arose. His longer, more complicated sentences became his standard type of writing in this period. The important works are "The Pupil," 1891; *What Maisie Knew*, 1897; and *The Turn of the Screw*, 1898.

5. 1900s: F. O. Matthiessen, a critic, gave this first decade of the twentieth century the name "The Major Phase," and the title is apt. James in this period, with an enormous burst of energy, wrote three major novels: *The Ambassadors*, 1903, but completed in 1901; *The Wings of the Dove*, 1902; and *The Golden Bowl*, 1904. These are James's maturest efforts; they are complex, massive, and difficult novels, but they are among the best in our language. It was during this period that James began editing his own novels and writing his "Prefaces," which are essays on the problems in writing his works and

studies of the novel as art, for the New York Edition of his works.

6. Final Phase: James left two unfinished works at his death: *The Sense of the Past*, 1917; *The Ivory Tower*, 1917.

MAJOR THEMES IN JAMES'S FICTION

Like all writers, James is concerned with the human situation, he is interpreting characters and life. When one refers to the major **themes** of a particular writer, he is thinking of those subjects and preoccupations that persist in a writer, that appear in many, if not most, of his works. The critic R. P. Blackmur, in *The Literary History of the United States*, distinguishes three **themes** in James's fiction: "international theme," the **theme** of the artist in conflict with society, and "the theme of the pilgrim in search of society." One can see that society is basic to James's works; he is constantly evaluating what one society maintains as its values and how these values affect groups and individuals. Many times he contrasts that particular society with the activities and mores of another society. Basically, the two societies that persist in his works are those of America and Europe.

Two dominant images emerge, therefore, in the fiction:

THE INNOCENT

James usually poses an innocent figure. The person is not stupid, not unintelligent. What James means in an innocent person is one who has not been touched by deep experience in worldly matters. These innocents are eager for life and they usually see life in others as an object for their own desires. Usually, in a

James novel, these intelligent and eager creatures are corrupted and spoiled by the sophisticated ones in whom the innocents think that the virtues they would like reside. The innocents are candid, and human. They have strength and respond with deep conviction when they see their ideals corrupted. They are almost always intelligent, and they naturally, without affectation, understand good and evil, right and wrong. The sophisticated ones prey on these innocents, because they substitute experience in the world for natural decency. However, the successes of the experienced are hollow. The strong figures in James are the natural good ones.

THE INTERNATIONAL THEME

Most of the things said about the heroes and heroines of a Jamesian work apply to this basic **theme** that James mastered and matured. The international subject is the study of the American abroad. These Americans are unaware of the **conventions** and formalities of Europe; they make mistakes, they have deficiencies intact and polish, but they have freedom, innocence, and grace, and these more than make up for their lack of experience. James contrasts the two societies very carefully: the American is not yet matured and he is awkward because he does not know how the society he is in expresses itself. He knows that there are deeper and lasting values in the society of Europe, but his natural way is usually in conflict with these values. Europe, on the other hand, does not have the vitality and youthfulness of the American world. Europe is a matter of **convention**, that is, formal responses in social situations. Every move, every act, is deliberate and committed in an established way. In James's last works, Europe does seem to represent an ideal, but the innocent, vital American remains a serious threat to the established order.

If one will examine in the following pages Henry James's *Daisy Miller*, he will see one of James's earliest examinations of the international **theme**. It is surprisingly a very full look at the whole subject in its basic forms. *Daisy Miller* looks forward to *The Portrait of a Lady* and the great accomplishment in the character of Isabel Archer and also to *The Wings of the Dove* and the more complete and subtle characterization of Milly Theale. These later works are more complicated, more difficult in style, but *Daisy Miller* presents the essential ideas inherent in the international theme.

Daisy, as a character, is an innocent, but the whole problem of innocence, especially in contrast to the influence of evil, comes out most vividly in *The Turn of the Screw*. There the entire story examines the potential meanings, the ironies and ambiguities, of this basic **theme**. Together *The Turn of the Screw* and *Daisy Miller* are two of Henry James's most popular stories. They contain his essential **themes** and his essential style. They are a good place for all students of James to begin.

THE JAMESIAN NOVEL

Henry James looked upon the novel as a work of art. In the truest sense of the word art, one can say James was one of the first writers to think of the novel in this way. James did not use the novel as a social document or as a forum for his philosophy. To James, the novel is a form complete in itself. Admittedly, he is difficult to read. The following is a synopsis of what one can expect to find in his works: First, a Jamesian novel is not a vehicle for something else. The story, plot, dialogue are complete within the work itself. Second, in a James novel, there is always what James referred to as the "central consciousness," that is, a mind and person through whom the story is being presented to the reader. James is always conscious of how the reader is hearing and seeing his story. Basically, he stays away from the omniscient narrator except for occasional comments. The omniscient narrator means that the story is told from the point of view of the author. He knows all the characters and what they are thinking and doing. James usually attempts to tell the story from the point of view of a character in the work. *In The Turn of the Screw*, James tells the story from the point of view of the first person narrator. In *Daisy Miller*, the story is seen through the mind of Winterbourne. The reader can note there that the story is never seen from Daisy's point of view. The story is about how Daisy is seen by others, especially Winterbourne. The reader should understand that James's dominating technical device is point of view, the decision that the author had made on from whose eyes, ears, and mind he is going to tell the story to the reader. Third, the reader soon realizes that in James's novels there are rarely, if ever, plain ornaments. Dialogue is never just plain talk; it is always moving the plot forward. Description always establishes a scene so that one can understand the direction of the work. Scenes are always full of meaning in relation to other things in the novel. Fourth, one can summarize all the above by saying that a Jamesian novel is always organic, all things are in relation to the whole. Nothing, not character, plot, story, scene, dialogue, description-nothing is isolated. All parts are related.

JAMES'S CRITICISM ON THE NOVEL

During his writing career James wrote many reviews, essays, and articles on writers and their works, but he made an outstanding contribution to the study of the novel in two separate parts of critical writings. First, from 1907 to 1917 there was issued a collected edition of Henry James's works. Usually this edition is referred to as "The New York Edition" by James scholars. For this collection, James selected the works, chose to leave some of his less successful works out (although some of these, such as *The Bostonians*, are considered highly now), revised passages in the works, and for each volume wrote a critical preface. These prefaces contain some of the most sophisticated discussions of the art of the novel in all literature. Usually, in each preface James tried to explain how he came upon the story, what he referred to as the "germ." Then James explained what possibilities he saw in the germ and the problems he was confronted with in developing the novel. In many cases James pointed to outstanding devices, techniques, and in many other cases James pointed out some of the mistakes he felt he had made. There are further discussions of the prefaces to *The Turn of the Screw* and *Daisy Miller*. These essays are surely among the most important documents on prose fiction, for they give an insight not only into the mind of a great writer, they also reveal the art of the novel.

Second, in September, 1884, James published in *Longman's*, a magazine, an essay known as "The Art of Fiction." It was written in reply to a lecture given by a Walter Besant, a Victorian novelist and historian. Besant's lecture, "Fiction as a Fine Art," has been forgotten except by literary scholars, but James's essay has remained one of the most important studies on the art of fiction. One must realize that James was a forerunner of the present thought that the novel can be looked upon as a serious work of art. Some of the more important aspects of the essay are as follows: 1. "The only reason for the existence of a novel is that it does attempt to represent life." He goes on to say that the "novel is history." 2. "The only obligation to which in advance we may hold a novel . . . is that it be interesting." James then adds that the ways to make a novel interesting are innumerable. 3. "A novel is in its broadest definition a personal, a direct impression of life: that, to begin with, constitutes its value, which is greater or less according to the intensity of the impression." 4. James agrees that a novel cannot be written without a deep sense of reality, but the reality must come from an awareness of the extent of experience. In a famous **metaphor** James explains experience: "Experience is never limited . . . ; it is an immense sensibility, a kind of huge spider-web of the finest silken threads suspended in the chamber of the consciousness, and catching every airborne particle in its tissue." 5. James refers to the novel as a "living thing." In other words, it is organic. (See under the Jamesian novel.) 6. According to James, there can be no distinction between character and incident. These are complements of each other. 7. Finally, James states one of the most quoted critical ideas in the essay: "We must grant the artist his subject, his idea, his donnee: our criticism is applied only to what he makes of it." There are many other items in both the "Art of Fiction" and the "Prefaces," but the student should be aware that most of the modern terms we use about the novel, the criticism that we apply to the novel, the serious manner in which we view the novel - these and other ideas had their most serious first statement in the criticism of Henry James.

THE TURN OF THE SCREW

INTRODUCTION

....

Henry James's horror tale, *The Turn of the Screw*, is one of his popular short novels and ranks with *Daisy Miller* among his most read works. James wrote this work late in his career during a time when he was examining the effects of evil as a presence in contrast to good. In this same period, James was already a very sophisticated and complex stylist. This work looks forward to the last great novels that he wrote, the novels usually referred to as constituting James's "major phase."

The late, complex style of James adds a dimension to *The Turn of the Screw*. On a very simple level, the story looks and reads like a simple horror tale being told by a woman who experienced the events. As the reader sees, however, this simple tale is so deliberately and carefully presented that almost every fact, every incident, every character, and every motive can have a second, and just as valid, interpretation by the reader. This is what is usually referred to as the "ambiguity" in *The Turn of the Screw*.

The following study guide of the story takes into account this problem of ambiguity. In the detailed summary, in which the introductory chapter and the following twenty-four chapters, are individually summarized, the possible double readings of all incidents are noted and discussed.

BRIEF SUMMARY OF THE STORY

At a gathering in an old English house, a group of people had just listened to a horror tale involving a child when a man named Douglas informed the others that he knew a story that involved two children. At the insistence of the others, Douglas sent a messenger for a manuscript that had been left him by a governess of his sister many years ago. As a background to the tale, Douglas told the people that the governess, the youngest daughter of a country parson, had at the age of twenty years answered an advertisement in the paper for a position. She met the advertiser, a handsome and rich bachelor living in an expensive home in London. He told her that the position involved the care of a young girl and also her brother when he was at home from boarding school. The only condition he stipulated was that the governess assume complete responsibility and not bother him at all. The governess, infatuated over the uncle, accepted. After this background, Douglas read the governess' manuscript.

The governess was greeted at Bly by Mrs. Grose, a servant, and the eight-year-old girl Flora. The child was beautiful, and the governess was reassured, but on her first evening at Bly she felt some unrest. The boy, Miles, was to come home from school within two days. On the day before his arrival, however, the governess received from the uncle an unopened letter from Miles's headmaster. The letter informed the governess that Miles had been dismissed from school and would not be allowed to return in the fall. The governess was puzzled over what the boy could have done. She assumed that he was a bad influence on the others, but her fears were allayed when Miles arrived and she found that he was a beautiful and innocent ten-year-old child.

At first the governess was charmed by the beautiful children, but one day while she was strolling by herself on the grounds of Bly she saw an unfamiliar figure standing on one of the towers of the large house and staring at her. The governess said nothing to anyone, but a few days later on a Sunday when she entered a room to get her gloves to wear at church, she saw at the window the face of the same man. Again, she was stunned, and this time she ran outside to find the unfamiliar person. But there was no one there. Mrs. Grose, surprised to see the governess outside in poor weather, appeared and asked what was the matter. The governess described carefully the man she saw, and immediately the servant recognized the man as Peter Quint, a former worker on the place. But Mrs. Grose added that Peter Quint was dead.

What bothered the governess most was the decision that she had made on this second appearance of the man; that he was not looking for her, but for Miles. A short time later the governess saw another ghost. This time she was sitting by a small lake sewing while Flora was playing with some pieces of wood a short distance away. The governess looked across the lake and saw a sad-looking woman. When she discussed this appearance with Mrs. Grose, it was clear that the woman was the predecessor of the governess, a Miss Jessel, who had finally left Bly and inexplicably died. The governess was sure that Flora had seen the woman but had feigned that she had not. She concluded that the children were lost and in league with the ghosts.

The governess tried to get all the information she could from Mrs. Grose, but the servant could give only few details. For a time the ghosts did not appear, but one night the governess felt a presence so she got up from bed. At the head of the stairway she saw Quint a third time but he disappeared quickly. When she returned to her room, she saw that Flora, who slept there also, was not in her bed. The girl appeared from near the window. The governess had a hard time believing that the child was simply playing a prank on her.

One evening, some days later, the governess again saw that Flora was out of her bed and leaning on the window sill looking down on the lawn. The governess stole out of the room and expected to find Quint and Miss Jessel outside, but to her horror she found that Flora was looking down at Miles. By that time, the governess was convinced that the children were subject to the evil of the ghosts and had been corrupted by them in the past.

One Sunday morning, the governess walked to church with the children, and after a few words with Miles decided that she would return to the house alone, clear up her things, and leave Bly. When she got to the house, she found Miss Jessel in the schoolroom. This caused the governess to give up her idea of leaving. She and Mrs. Grose decided it was time to write to the uncle, however reluctant they were to take that extreme measure. With great difficulty the governess wrote the note and left it on a table for a servant to take into the village

On a particularly wet day, the governess realized that Flora was not in the house. The governess went directly to Mrs. Grose and went outside with her to the lake to find the little girl. Mrs. Grose was somewhat surprised at the governess's actions. The child was not on the near side of the lake; instead of turning back, the governess walked to the other side where, as she had anticipated, they found Flora. Unable to restrain herself any longer, the governess asked the child where Miss Jessel was. The governess could see the wretched woman on the other side of the lake. The child responded with horror, and although the governess insisted, even Mrs. Grose said that she saw no one at all by the lake. The governess returned to the house alone, but to her very great relief, Mrs. Grose came to her the next morning and told her that, although the child was feverish and agitated she, the servant, now believed what the governess was saying all along on the basis of some of the things the child was saying in her delirium. The two women decided that Mrs. Grose should leave Bly with Flora and leave the governess alone with Miles, so that the governess could finally save the young boy from the evil of the ghosts.

The governess left Miles alone that day after Mrs. Grose and Flora had departed. At dinner in the evening, the governess and Miles had their chance. The boy asked about his sister, but the governess felt that they were talking around the thing on their minds. Finally, the boy confessed that he had removed the governess's letter to his uncle and read it. He then admitted that he had been saying things to his friends at school. The governess saw that the ghost of Peter Quint was there at the window. At first she protected Miles from the ghost, for she felt that she was in a battle with a demon for the soul of the boy. Eventually, the governess hugged the boy and caused him to ask if Miss Jessel were there. The boy was greatly upset, and the governess forced him to say the name of Peter Quint. The boy said, "Peter Quint- you devil," but did not see him. He asked where the man was. The governess pointed and tried to show the child, but Miles fell into her arms. He had died.

THE TURN OF THE SCREW

TEXTUAL ANALYSIS

INTRODUCTORY CHAPTER

A story about a ghost's appearing to a little boy in an old house had just held the attention of a gathering on Christmas eve in an old house like the one in the story. It seems, as narrated by the author (more specifically, an "I" in the novel), that the boy in the story woke up his mother, sleeping in the same room, to confront the same apparition. It was this aspect of the story that caused a man named Douglas, one of the people gathered, to make a reply (one that would lead into the tale to follow). The narrator knew Douglas had something on his mind, just by the way he paid no attention to the next storyteller, but that something would come out two days later.

However, on that same evening, Douglas did comment that the appearance of a ghost to a child was certainly a deepening of a story (another "turn of the screw," that is, a complication asserted). Then he asked the group what they would think if there were two children involved. Someone explained that that would be "two turns."

Douglas, with the rest of the gathering quite excited, admitted that he had a story that went "beyond everything" for "dreadfulness," for "ugliness and horror and pain." Douglas was asked to begin the story immediately, but he explained that it was locked up in a drawer in his home and that he could send for it. The narrator asked Douglas if he himself were involved in the experience. Douglas answered, "thank God, no" The manuscript he had had been written and left to him by a woman now dead twenty years. This woman was ten years older than he and was his sister's governess, years after the events of the narration had taken place. Douglas met the governess when he came home one summer from school. He confessed that he liked her very much and thought she liked him.

The governess had never told the story before because "she was in love." When asked with whom, Douglas said that the story would reveal that but "not in any literal, vulgar way." The people present wanted to hear more, but Douglas told them they would have to wait. On the next evening, Douglas became communicative because his manuscript needed a few words of prologue. (The narrator explains that he is writing this section from an "exact transcript." Later, the narrator says, Douglas on his death bed left him the manuscript.)

Douglas filled in the following details as a background for the narrative: The governess was the youngest daughter of a poor country parson. She had come to London at the age of twenty to answer an advertisement in the paper. In a very imposing house on Harley Street, she met a bachelor "in the prime of life," the man who had placed the advertisement. The bachelor struck the governess as being the type of man she dreamed of or a man who would appear in an old novel. To her, he was handsome and gallant, very rich and fearfully extravagant. This bachelor had become guardian to his small nephew and niece, children of his younger brother, who had died two years before in India. The uncle was greatly concerned over the young children, but his own affairs occupied much of his time. He had placed them in his house, named Bly, with an excellent housekeeper, Mrs. Grose. There were other servants and workers, but the governess would become the head of the household. She would have to be prepared to take care of the young nephew Miles when he came home from school. Miles had been sent to boarding school at his young age because the young lady who took care of the children had come to misfortune. The niece, Flora, was left in the care of Mrs. Grose.

When Douglas had given this much information, he was asked what the previous governess had died of. Douglas answered that they would find out the next evening. The governess thought over the position. One of the gathering conjectured that she took the position because of the young bachelor. Douglas replied that she saw him only twice. That, added another, was what made her passion so important. Douglas agreed and then stated that the bachelor had one main condition that the governess had to meet: that the governess completely take over and never bother him. She agreed. After that meeting, she never saw him again.

Then someone asked Douglas if he had a title to his story. He said, he did not. The narrator said he had one, but Douglas had already begun to read the manuscript.

Comment

If one is to read the story very carefully, he will note that there is much information given in this introductory chapter. James rarely wrote a prologue to his works, for he believed that his novels and tales were organic, all things related to one another. Here, however, James uses his introduction to the tale to show

how the manuscript came into being and how the story was told. He is able to give the background to the governess, who will tell the tale. Since what follows is a first person narrative, it would have been awkward and artificial to invent a circumstance for her to tell her age and where she was born, for example. The author is also able to comment on the young governess through the character of Douglas who had known her many years before.

The statements about the impressions that the governess had of the uncle of the children in the story must have been related to Douglas originally by the governess herself. These are the only words about the uncle except that the governess will constantly think about him throughout her tale and he will be a constant, but distant, presence in the work. See summary of Chapter III, for example, where the governess sees the first ghost in the story. She will be thinking that she would like to see the uncle of the children at that time.

The background of the governess has been considered very important by many readers. Her being the youngest daughter of a country parson and being in the position of a governess, some feel, distinguish her as a spinster type, with only an imaginative involvement in life, rather than experience in life. One should also consider the position of Douglas in the story. He, who has known the governess, considers her the "most agreeable" woman he has known. Apparently, he has liked her very much although she was ten years older than he. The reader should keep this in mind as he reads her story.

One final observation about the summary of the chapter. The reader should note that the gathering is prepared to hear a ghost story, or, more accurately, a "horror" story. The question throughout the story is the dread that the governess feels, whether it be in her mind or actually exists.

THE TURN OF THE SCREW

TEXTUAL ANALYSIS

CHAPTER I

Note: The reader knows from the summary of the introductory chapter that Douglas is reading a manuscript. The actual story of *The Turn of the Screw* is a first person narrative. The governess, whose name is never given, is telling her own story. The summary of the following twenty-four chapters is conducted as a third person story. An attempt is made to remind the reader that the story is told exclusively from the point of view of the governess, but where the first person narrative is important for a particular interpretation, detailed explanations are given in the comments which follow the chapter summaries.

The governess recalls her trip in a coach to Bly. She felt that she might have made a mistake in taking the position. She felt low, and she was surprised to see the house was a pleasant looking place, quite large compared to her own home. She was met at the door by a little girl holding the hand of a servant. That little girl, Flora, introduced by Mrs. Grose, was "the most beautiful child" she had ever seen. The governess was elated.

She felt that Flora was so happy that she was straining not to show it. That evening, the governess did not sleep very well because she was thinking of the beautiful girl and the great pleasure she would have in educating her. Also, that evening, she thought she heard the faint, distant cry of a child and a light footstep outside her door. At any rate, she had decided that she liked Mrs. Grose already.

She asked the servant if the boy, Miles, were also "remarkable." Mrs. Grose finally told her that if she considered Flora remarkable, she would be carried away by the "little gentleman." Miles was to arrive from school on Friday of that week, and the governess said she would meet him with Flora and Mrs. Grose.

On the next day, because she had decided to make the little girl like her, the governess spent much time with Flora, who showed her around the place, its stairs, rooms, and passages. Now, the governess thought the place less wonderful than she did on that day when she made her first tour. She remembered that she realized that she was "at the helm," as she put it.

Comment

The governess's narrative begins quietly. She does not romanticize the house, Bly, when she comes to it. There are small adumbrations, hints, put before the reader, however, and one can note that a special tone in the governess's narrative is already sounded. When the governess meets Flora, she comments that the child is so happy to see her that she is trying hard to hide it. The reader cannot tell if this is so at all, for the child may be suspicious of the new governess. One notices how the governess is struck by the beauty of the child. So long as she thinks the little girl is innocent, she will think of her as beautiful. This will change significantly later in the tale.

Immediately, one can also note - and the reader should get accustomed to making these distinctions in the reading of the story - the ambiguity of the governess's first night in the house. Her feeling of discomfort, the thought that she hears a light footstep in the corridor, or the sound in the distance - these are important. If she is a neurotic person, then these are figments of her imagination. If she is accurate, then Bly is haunted. This type of distinction is very important for the reader.

THE TURN OF THE SCREW

TEXTUAL ANALYSIS

CHAPTER II

....

The governess's first full day had been reassuring, she said. But she received a letter from her employer explaining that he recognized the handwriting on an enclosed and unopened letter to be that of the headmaster at Mile's school and that he was bored with those notes. The uncle ordered the governess to act but not to report to him. Regretfully, the governess read the headmaster's note before she went to bed that evening and again could not sleep because of the contents.

Since she had no one to confide in, she said, she decided to speak to Mrs. Grose. She wanted to know why Miles would be dismissed from school and why they would refuse to take him back. Mrs. Grose asked what the young gentleman had done, but when the governess showed her the note, Mrs. Grose did not take it. (She cannot read.) The governess asked if Miles were "bad." The letter gave no details, but the governess said that it could only mean that the people at the school did not want him because he was "an injury to the others," to his "poor innocent mates," she said. Mrs. Grose said that that could not be because Miles was scarcely ten years old. She begged the governess to see for herself.

At that moment, little Flora was standing there although the governess had left her ten minutes before while she was doing some handwriting exercises. The governess took the little girl in her arms and covered her with kisses. Later that day, however, the governess again stopped Mrs. Grose and asked if Miles were the type to corrupt others. The servant slyly asked the young lady if she were afraid that Miles would corrupt her.

The next day, near the time to meet Miles, the governess asked about the lady who had preceded her. Mrs. Grose said that she was young and pretty, like the present one. The governess commented that "he" seemed to like his girls young and pretty. Mrs. Grose said, yes, her master did. The governess felt that Mrs. Grose was referring to someone else as "master." The governess asked about her predecessor's relationship with Miles. Mrs. Grose was reluctant to talk about that. Then the governess wanted to know how she died. Mrs. Grose explained that the young lady had left on one of her holidays and never returned. When the governess insisted on asking of what she died, Mrs. Grose pleaded that she had work to do and left.

Comment

The matter of Miles's dismissal from boarding school reappears in the governess's mind through the entire tale until the last chapter when she will confront the young boy with that fact and ask him to explain. No complete explanation is given.

One can decide that the governess comes to her conclusions about Miles much too rapidly, that she acts with suspicion and does not give the boy an opportunity to explain. Mrs. Grose, illiterate though she is, senses that no specific reason is given for Miles's dismissal.

The governess's concern to know all the details about her predecessor may be simply an honest desire to know or a revelation of her morbid attitude toward her new position.

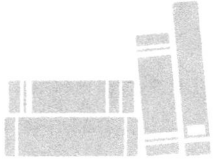

THE TURN OF THE SCREW

TEXTUAL ANALYSIS

CHAPTER III

The governess went to meet Miles, and she reports in her manuscript that she thought him "incredibly beautiful." She felt that he had an "indescribable little air of knowing nothing in the world but love." At Bly, she told Mrs. Grose that the servant was right in her opinion of Miles, that the charges in the letter from the headmaster were grotesque and that she herself would say nothing to the headmaster in reply, or to the uncle and Miles. The two women, overjoyed, embraced and kissed.

As she reflected back on that time, the governess was puzzled at her reaction. She was trapped, she declared, and off guard because the children were extraordinarily gentle. It was this that made what followed seem "like the spring of a beast." The governess enjoyed her private hour when she was alone after the children were in bed. One afternoon on her normal stroll, her mind lingered on the thought of seeing a man she wanted to see. When she came out of the woods and into view of the house, she saw standing at the top of one of the towers by Bly, that Flora had shown her on her first day there, the man she wanted to see. But the figure there was not the one she was thinking about at all, but altogether another man. It was not the face she had seen in Harley Street.

While the two stared at each other, the governess went over in her mind all the possibility of who the figure could be. But it was an unfamiliar man who stood and stared right at her, she said, walked from one side of the balcony to the other, continued his gaze at her, and then walked away.

Comment

The governess at first associates Miles with innocence. She emphasizes how beautiful he is, just as she did with his sister. The governess is always ready to speak in extremes, the reader soon sees.

This first appearance of Peter Quint is very important. There is no way to know if the ghost is really there or not, but probably the reader should accept what the governess says. Her state of mind is very important, however. As she is strolling alone, she is thinking exclusively of the uncle. She wants to see him. When she sees the figure on the balcony, she at first assumes that it is the uncle, the bachelor, who so infatuated her. One notes that she goes over other possible people before she decides that it is an unfamiliar person. The question might be put in this way: does the governess dream up the vision?

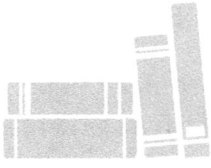

THE TURN OF THE SCREW

TEXTUAL ANALYSIS

CHAPTER IV

....

The governess thought over this incident "in a confusion of curiosity and dread." She realized that she was feeling fear when she did not mention anything about it to Mrs. Grose after she returned to the house that evening. The governess thought that she had been made the object of a game by the servants. She forgot herself, however, in the activity of educating the children. She knew that she was right in her decision that Miles could not have done the wrong that the letter from the headmaster indicated. He was a "beautiful" boy, and the governess was dazzled by the children's loveliness.

One Sunday afternoon, after a heavy rain had stopped and given them an opportunity to go to the evening church service, the governess came downstairs and went into a room to get a pair of gloves. When she entered the room, she saw, looking in from the wide window, the very same man she had seen on the balcony. Again, she saw him from the waist up. He was there only a few seconds, but the governess was convinced that she had known him for years. This time, however, the man did not stare at the young lady only, but also cast his glance from object to object in the room. The governess was shocked when she realized that he had come for someone else, not her.

This thought shocked the governess, but it also gave her courage. In a short time, she ran out the door and on to the terrace, but there was no one there. She went to the same window and looked inside and saw there Mrs. Grose. Mrs. Grose was startled.

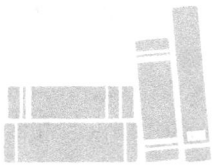

THE TURN OF THE SCREW

TEXTUAL ANALYSIS

CHAPTER V

Mrs. Grose came around the corner of the house and asked the governess what was the matter with her because she was as white as a sheet. The governess told the servant that she had seen an "extraordinary man looking in." Mrs. Grose asked her if she had seen him before, and the governess told her that she had seen him once before on the tower. The governess told the servant that the man was no "gentleman" but a "horror." She was afraid to go to church now because she wanted to protect the children, and she was afraid of the man.

Mrs. Grose for the first time gave a hint of understanding something. She asked the governess when she had seen the man before, and how she had the nerve to go out after him. Finally, the servant asked what the man was like. The governess gave a detailed description: "He has red hair, very red, close-curling, and a pale face . . . with straight, good features, and little, rather queer whiskers . . . his eyebrows . . . look particularly arched . . . his eyes are sharp, strange . . . his mouth's wide, and his lips are thin . . . and he's quite clean-shaven. He gives me a sort of sense of looking like an actor."

Mrs. Grose recognized the description, asked if he were handsome, to which the governess replied, he was. She knew that he did not look like a gentleman because the clothes that he wore were not his, but his master's. Mrs. Grose said that it was, "Quint," Peter Quint, the master's valet, had been alone at Bly with the servant and the children after the uncle had left. The governess asked what became of him. Mrs. Grose said that he had left. Then she said, "Mr. Quint is dead."

Comment

The second appearance of Peter Quint is the important one, for at this point the reader realizes that the tale has turned into a ghost story. The matter of interpretation, however, is altogether a much more difficult problem that the reader must resolve. Since only the governess sees the figure, the question one must ask is whether the ghost actually appears or not.

First, it is obvious that the governess's description is vividly detailed. She captures all the facial features, she knows the clothes, and she interprets. Mrs. Grose recognizes Peter Quint immediately. It would seem that the governess has actually seen a figure and seen it clearly. The governess further recognizes that the ghost is looking for someone else. She knows that would be Miles.

For those who would assume that this evidence is strong enough to prove that the ghosts to appear and are not just a matter of the governess's imagination, perhaps they should note that several important studies claim otherwise. The point of the matter is that the governess, who has already shown a particular eagerness to know about the past servants and who walks around with visions of the uncle, has also been talking to the villagers. That comes out in the next chapter of the novel, if one reads carefully, and also how she has found out the way that Quint died.

At any rate though this chapter is probably as ambiguous as the rest of the novel, it is one of the important ones that must be considered if one is to make a complete interpretation.

THE TURN OF THE SCREW

TEXTUAL ANALYSIS

CHAPTER VI

That evening the governess and Mrs. Grose did not attend church services. Mrs. Grose had not seen anything, but she accepted everything that the governess said as true. The two, according to the governess, decided "to bear things together." After they had gone over and over everything that the governess had seen, she finally exclaimed that the figure was looking for Miles. Mrs. Grose was surprised at this, but the governess was convinced. She was also concerned that the children had not mentioned Peter Quint to her Mrs. Grose explained that Flora was too young to have known him, and the friendship between Miles and Quint was a matter of the latter's being "too free" with the young boy. The governess concluded that Quint was admittedly bad, but Mrs. Grose said the master, meaning the uncle, did not know that. She had not said anything to him because she feared the man.

The governess was sure that Mrs. Grose had held something back that Sunday evening. For her own part the governess was sure that she knew what everything had been like and that the evil of Quint had ended when he was found dead by a villager on the road from the local town. The governess had difficulty explaining her state of mind at that time, but she decided that she was going to succeed where her predecessor had failed, that she was going to protect the innocent and bereaved children. She said, "we were united in danger."

But an incident took place that cast a new light on the whole matter. One afternoon, leaving Miles indoors to finish reading a book, the governess and Flora went out to stroll about the grounds. They came to a small lake. The governess, so thrilled with her position, imagined that she and Flora were beside the Sea of Azof. Suddenly, she became aware that there was someone on the other side of the lake. She continued her sewing as she sat, but she was sure that there was no doubt that she could see the figure across the way. Then she turned her eyes to little Flora who was playing close by. She expected the child to give a cry or something, but nothing came. Flora had a small piece of wood, which had in it a small hole, and the little girl had evidently decided on sticking another piece of wood in the hole and making a mast for a play boat. Finally, the governess, who had kept her eyes on her stitching, decided to face the figure on the other side of the lake.

Comment

It is with this appearance of the second ghost, the former governess, Miss Jessel, that the real complications in the interpretation of the story begin. The governess states that she is sure that she saw the figure of the woman. For the moment, one can leave that fact, but one should note that the child Flora is playing with two pieces of wood, probably innocent play. (For comment on these pieces of wood, see the essay by Edmund Wilson in the Critical Commentary.) Again, in other words, only the governess for sure sees the ghost. The significance of understanding this comes out in the next chapter when the governess speaks to Mrs. Grose.

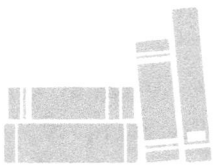

THE TURN OF THE SCREW

TEXTUAL ANALYSIS

CHAPTER VII

....

As soon as she could, with considerable trouble restraining herself, the governess spoke with Mrs. Grose and told her that the children knew everything, everything that the two of them knew. When Mrs. Grose expressed surprise, the governess explained that Flora had seen the figure in the garden and had not said a word. The figure was a "horror and evil: a woman in black, pale and dreadful." The governess said that it had to be her predecessor. Mrs. Grose could not believe that it was Miss Jessel, but the governess insisted that Flora knew she was there and did not want her companion to know. The servant was visibly upset when the governess told her that the woman had fixed her gaze on Flora and wanted her.

The governess forced Mrs. Grose into some explanations. The servant said that Miss Jessel was a lady, but Quint had hounded her, as he had everyone else, although he was of lower class. He did what he wished "with them all." The governess wanted to know how Miss Jessel had died. Mrs. Grose simply said that she could not stay at Bly any longer and had to leave and that she personally could imagine why she had to leave. The governess, who made interpretations of everything the servant said, knew that there was something very dreadful involved. The children, she had decided, were "lost."

Comment

The pattern of the story of the governess is now fully established in this chapter. The ambiguity, the possible double reading of the entire work, is clear.

The governess has now decided that the children know everything. She is convinced that Flora saw the ghost, Miss Jessel, but feigned not seeing her. She decides that the children are lost, for the ghosts are after the children, not after the governess. If the governess is right, then her conclusion is right. The story is the development of the governess's desire to protect the children and save them from the evil intent of the two former corrupters who have returned to claim the children.

The other point of view is just as telling, for the reader is justifiably surprised with the definite and assured way in which the governess has decided that the figure she saw was her predecessor. Once again, we have a puzzling fact. Once again, the reader cannot be sure if the governess is making everything up and that she will ultimately corrupt the children.

THE TURN OF THE SCREW

TEXTUAL ANALYSIS

CHAPTER VIII

....

Late that evening, the two women had a talk again, and this time the governess explained that if she were making up what she saw, Mrs. Grose would not have been able to recognize her descriptions so readily.

When she left Mrs. Grose, the governess went to the children, and although Flora greeted her by telling her that she must have been crying, the governess was sure that she had not revealed any of the things that she now knew. The event of the afternoon had caused her to review all the details. Late that night, she once again went to Mrs. Grose and wanted a more complete explanation of why she responded the way she did when she, the governess, had shown her the letter from the headmaster. Why had she insisted that Miles could do no such wrong, the governess wanted to know. Mrs. Grose revealed that she had questioned the propriety of Miles's being with Mr. Quint so much (since he was a "base menial," the governess interjects), Miles had subsequently denied that he was with Quint on several occasions, (He "lied," said the governess.) According to Mrs. Grose, Miss Jessel did not forbid Miles to see the man. At any event, continued the servant, when Miles was with Quint, Flora was with Miss Jessel. "It suited them." The governess's conclusions bothered Mrs. Grose, but the governess said that she would have to wait.

Comment

Mrs. Grose is the true innocent in the tale. In this chapter, the governess keeps up with her persistence in finding out all she can.

THE TURN OF THE SCREW

TEXTUAL ANALYSIS

CHAPTER IX

....

The governess waited and waited for further signs, and she constantly wondered if her sudden shows of emotion for the children, when she passionately hugged them or kissed them impulsively, would reveal that she had suspicions about them. She was sure that the children were very fond of her at this time. "We lived in a cloud of music and love and success and private theatricals." Of course, the governess did think of the matter of a new school for Miles since he could not return to his former one, but she did not bring the subject up.

This description of that particular time, the governess said, was a prelude to a time after which the entire affair became "pure suffering." One evening, she was in bed reading a novel, Henry Fielding's *Amelia*, when she felt somewhat as she had on the first night she spent in the house. She laid down her book, took a candle, went out into the corridor, and closed the door quietly. She walked to the head of the staircase. There her candle went out, and she realized that she was seeing Quint halfway up the stairs. She said that he recognized her and knew that she had no fear of him. The "living, detestable, dangerous presence" finally turned and walked back into the darkness.

THE TURN OF THE SCREW

TEXTUAL ANALYSIS

CHAPTER X

When she knew that the man had left, the governess returned to her room, but once there, she realized that although the curtain was pulled around the bed Flora was not in her bed. As she came to the child's bed, she saw her coming from the window. The child told her that she had sensed that her governess was not in the room and had gone to the window to look outside for her. She had drawn the curtain, Flora said, so as not to upset the governess. She had not seen anyone. At this point, the governess felt the great temptation to bring everything out into the open with the girl, to accuse her of knowing everything. But she thought the better of that.

The governess related in her story that she never saw Quint in the house again, but she did see Miss Jessel sitting on one of the lower steps of the staircase, her head bowed in an attitude of woe. Although she could not see the face, the governess knew that it would be dreadful. On the eleventh night after seeing Quint - the governess reported that she had taken to counting the days-she awoke from her sleep at one o'clock in the morning and saw that Flora was not in bed. She saw the child at the window sill, apparently absorbed with staring at someone on the lawn. The governess was sure that the child had given herself over to Miss Jessel. As she stole out of the room, she was greatly tempted to see if Miles were in his bed, but she went instead to an empty room that would give her a view outside, an empty room on a lower level. There, when she looked out of the window, she was sure that someone was standing on the tower, but to her great surprise - "I felt sick as I made it out," she said - the figure standing on the lawn was no other than that of Miles.

THE TURN OF THE SCREW

TEXTUAL ANALYSIS

CHAPTER XI

....

Because she kept such a close guard over her pupils, the governess did not get a chance to tell Mrs. Grose about the incident until very late the next day. The governess was sure that Mrs. Grose believed her, but the servant was a "magnificent monument to the blessing of a want of imagination." The governess reached the point in her recitation to Mrs. Grose when she went down for Miles on the lawn. She simply took his hand and walked inside with him. Not a word passed between them. The governess wondered how Miles would try to get out of it, as she put it. When they got to his room, the governess knew that Miles "had" her. Mrs. Grose could never understand it. Finally, the governess, kindly and mercifully, as she put it, wanted to know from the young boy why he had gone outside. He told her he had done so just so that she would think him "bad." He had arranged with his sister for her to put out the light because he knew that the governess would respond just the way she did. The interview ended when the woman embraced the young boy and recognized the goodness of the boy.

Comment

This incident and those in the preceding two chapters are important in the tale. After the governess has seen Quint again, she becomes even more suspicious of the children. From her point of view, the children are in league with the two ghosts. She feels that the children are lost, have been corrupted by the ghosts in the past. As always, the reader can take another point of view. The children may be involved in a simple game of deception because they know that the governess is watching them closely, just as Miles says they are. Of course, the governess's impulsive embracing of Miles after he gives his explanation is perfectly in keeping with her excitable nature.

THE TURN OF THE SCREW

TEXTUAL ANALYSIS

CHAPTER XII

In the morning, however, the governess told Mrs. Grose that all the things Miles was saying were lies, that probably it was this that he had done in school. The governess had not changed her mind: she was simply beginning to understand things, she said. The children's goodness and proper behavior were a plot and a fraud, she said to Mrs. Grose. The children had been leading their own lives; actually they belonged to Quint and the woman. When Mrs. Grose asked why, the governess said, "For the love of all the evils that the pair put into them." The demons were coming back to make the children keep up their evil work. The final success of the tempters, according to the governess, would come when the children would perish.

The only way that the whole affair could be prevented, she told the servant, was by writing to the uncle. Of course, she felt that Mrs. Grose should do that task, but the servant interpreted it as meaning that the uncle should come for the governess. At that, the governess said that she would leave Bly if the servant called the master.

THE TURN OF THE SCREW

TEXTUAL ANALYSIS

CHAPTER XIII

The governess was convinced that the children knew that she sensed the truth. "It was not, I am as sure today as I was sure then, my mere infernal imagination." Since running across Quint on the staircase and Miss Jessel sitting there, the governess had not seen the two and her nerves were somewhat soothed. She expected to run across them in many, many places, but for the time they did not appear. At times when she was with the children, she was sure that they were seeing the figures and she was ready to scream out, but she did not. More than anything else, she was frightened by the evening when she saw Miles on the lawn instead of Quint. The children, in the meantime, acted as they always did; they must have been adorable at that time, the governess wrote in her manuscript, for her not to have hated them.

Comment

The reader realizes by this point in the novel that the children might be innocently playing and that the governess's imagination has taken over her rational evaluation of their behavior.

THE TURN OF THE SCREW

TEXTUAL ANALYSIS

CHAPTER XIV

On the way to church one Sunday, the governess was walking with Miles at her side, while Flora and Mrs. Grose went ahead. Then Miles began to talk with the governess-she called it in her manuscript, "the last act of my drama, and the **catastrophe** was precipitated-about himself. First he asked when in the world he would be going back to school. He said that it was not right for a "fellow to be with a lady always."

He admitted that the lady he was with "was perfect," but he felt that he had been good, except for the night when he had gone out on the lawn, and now he wanted to return to school. The governess asked him if he were not happy, and he answered that he was but that there was more he wanted to see. When she asked what, the young boy answered "more life." He wanted to be with his own sort (meaning boys).

The governess told him he was with his own sort when he was with Flora, but Miles did not like being compared to a "baby girl," as he put it. Then he asked what his uncle thought of his behavior, if he thought as his governess did. The governess confessed that she thought that the uncle did not care much about him. Miles thought that his uncle might care if he came down to visit. The governess asked who would make him come. Miles said that he would.

Comment

The governess is convinced that everything that Miles says is deception, that he is actually skirting what he really wants to say. In many of these conversations, there can be no doubt that the governess is pressing the young boy, for however precocious he is, he cannot know that the governess is interpreting all his remarks as though he had further meanings.

THE TURN OF THE SCREW

TEXTUAL ANALYSIS

CHAPTER XV

....

What Miles had said to the governess caused her to think of everything, and it prevented her from entering the church in such an agitated state. She walked around the church and stood under the window near the pew where the children would be sitting. She thought that since the arrival of the young boy, she had wanted to get away from him. This would be her chance to be alone in the house to do a few things, then to leave.

She walked back to the house. As she wrote the manuscript, she felt that she had decided to leave. When she got to the staircase, she recalled with revulsion that that was the place she had seen "the specter of the most horrible of women." She recovered herself and went up to the schoolroom where there were objects belonging to her. When she opened the door, she saw something that caused her to reel back.

Seated at her own table, she saw Miss Jessel. She was surveying the room and the things in it. She looked weary. She stood up, not from any sound, with a detached look, "dishonored and tragic," her black dress giving her the look of "unutterable woe," and it was at this point, the governess recorded, that she looked like herself. The governess felt like the intruder herself, and she heard herself say, "You terrible, miserable woman." Then the governess recovered herself. There was nothing in the room but the sunshine "and a sense that I must stay."

Comment

If one reads the novel as the quest of the governess to free the children from the evil of Quint and Jessel, then this must be considered the climactic moment in the story. It is after the governess has decided to leave that she sees Miss Jessel in the schoolroom and decides that she must stay. From this point on, she brings about the climactic moments of action in the story, but this must be the **climax** itself. After this, it is almost as if the governess has to force the crisis, is compelled to, in order to preserve her sanity and save the children.

THE TURN OF THE SCREW

TEXTUAL ANALYSIS

CHAPTER XVI

....

The governess had expected that she would see some demonstration on the part of the children because she had left them at church, but she was even more upset that they said nothing and made no sign when they saw her. She saw Mrs. Grose in the housekeeper's room before tea-time. The servant told her that the children had asked her to say nothing because they thought that their governess would want to be alone. Miles had said that they should do what would make her happy. The governess told Mrs. Grose that it was all out for her and Miles and that she had come home to have a "talk with Miss Jessel," or what amounted to a talk anyway. She told Mrs. Grose that she had found Miss Jessel in the schoolroom and her predecessor had told her "that she suffers the torments of the lost, of the damned." The governess added that "she wants Flora."

Then the governess told Mrs. Grose that she was prepared to get in touch with the uncle. She felt that she should have sent the letter from the headmaster to the uncle. But she was not sure of herself. Mrs. Grose said that she would communicate with the uncle, or that she would tell the bailiff to write for her. Of course, then there was the matter of the bailiff's knowing the story. The governess finally said she would write that night.

THE TURN OF THE SCREW

TEXTUAL ANALYSIS

CHAPTER XVII

....

She tried to start her letter that night, but she got up from the blank page before her, left the room, and stood listening at Miles's door. Miles's voice called out and asked what she was doing there, for he had heard her. When she entered the room, the governess asked him why he was not sleeping. He said that he was thinking about her and their relationship and "all the rest." The governess pressed him for explanations. She told him that he had never said a word about his former school, or his previous life, since he had returned.

Miles said he liked Bly, but he also wanted to get away for the reasons he had given in the morning. The governess brought up his uncle, and Miles told her that he would, of course, have much to tell him if he came down to Bly. The governess asked Miles what he would have to say to his uncle. She told the boy that she had begun a letter to his uncle, and the boy told her, nicely, to finish it. But she insisted in asking Miles if he had anything to tell her about "before you came back, and before you went away." Then she pressed him and pleaded with him, declaring that she wanted to help him. Suddenly, she felt a blast of cold air. Miles screamed. She jumped up in terror and cried that the candle was out. "It was I who blew it, dear!" said Miles.

THE TURN OF THE SCREW

TEXTUAL ANALYSIS

CHAPTER XVIII

....

The next day, Mrs. Grose asked her if she had written the letter. The governess replied that she had, but she had not posted it with the messenger to town as yet. The children at their lessons were particularly good that day. The governess was pleased. After an early dinner that day, Miles came to her and asked if she would like him to play for her that day. They went up to the schoolroom together and there Miles played the piano for her. When he finished, the governess asked him where Flora was, but Miles simply said that he did not know.

The governess immediately went up to her room to see if Flora were in bed. When she did not find her there, she went down to the housekeeper's room and asked Mrs. Grose where the child was. Mrs. Grose told her that the little girl would be in her room soon, that probably she was in one of the empty rooms in the house. The governess replied that Flora was out with Miss Jessel. When Mrs. Grose asked where Miles was, the governess added that Miles was in the schoolroom with Peter Quint. She said that the children had tricked her. She did not care now that she had written the note to the uncle. She took the note out and placed it on the table, saying that Luke would pick it up.

Then she made ready to go out. Mrs. Grose asked her if she should not wear something because it was wet and grey outside. The governess answered that she did not need anything if the little girl herself had gone out with nothing on. The governess could not wait.

Comment

At this point in the story, the reader can sense that the governess seems driven. These chapters are made much of by those who claim the story is one of a sexually repressed spinster.

THE TURN OF THE SCREW

TEXTUAL ANALYSIS

CHAPTER XIX

....

The governess led Mrs. Grose directly to the lake, to the same place where she was sure that little Flora had feigned that she had not seen Miss Jessel. The governess was sure that the child was there, and with the former governess. There was no trace of Flora when the two reached the lake, but the governess insisted that they go around to the other side of the water because she was sure that Flora had gone across in the boat and hidden it there. Mrs. Grose was shaken by this, but she went along.

Flora was on the other side of the lake. When they saw her, she smiled at them. The governess decided that she would not speak first, but Mrs. Grose broke the ice and embraced the child. Finally, Flora asked them why they did not have extra clothing. "Why, where are your things?" she asked. The governess took up the challenge, "Where yours are, my dear!"

Then the child asked after her brother. At this point, with Mrs. Grose "blazing" at her, the governess, as she put it in her manuscript, "brought the thing handsomely." "Where, my pet, is Miss Jessel?" she asked.

Comment

The governess seems almost demonic in the glee with which she has recorded this incident in her manuscript. Certainly, this is one of the important scenes that should be considered before one goes on to the next chapter for the sequence to the governess's bringing the entire matter out into the open. Once again, one must be reminded that such incidents can be read in two ways. If the governess is right, then she is trying to save the children. She must force the issue because she is striving against supernatural forces. If on the other hand the governess is so personally involved that she is only working out her frustrations, then she must be seen as the corrupter of the innocent children, in this case, the antagonizer of the bewildered child, Flora.

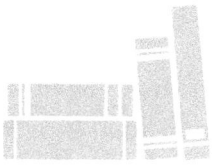

THE TURN OF THE SCREW

TEXTUAL ANALYSIS

CHAPTER XX

....

Now, the governess felt, the whole thing was out in the open as it was in the church yard with Miles. Mrs. Grose gave out a cry, but the governess seized her arms and said, "She's there, she's there!" The governess could see Miss Jessel on the other side of the lake, the place where she and Mrs. Grose had just come from. Mrs. Grose gazed and blinked as she looked across; it was positive that she could see the woman, said the governess. Flora, however, did not look to the place but right at the governess with an expression of judgment and accusation. The governess insisted that she knew Miss Jessel was there. Mrs. Grose at this point blotted out everything with her next comment, "what a dreadful turn, to be sure, Miss! Where on earth do you see anything?"

Even as Mrs. Grose was saying these words, the governess could see Miss Jessel, but she could also see that the servant was taking the side of the child. Mrs. Grose looked pained; she said, "nobody's there - and you never see nothing." She tried to call it all a mistake and a joke. Then little Flora cried out, "I don't know what you mean. I see nobody. I see nothing. I never have. I think you're cruel. I don't like you!" Flora wanted to be taken away from the governess.

Mrs. Grose went back to the house with the child. The governess did not recall exactly what she thought the few minutes she stood there alone. When she finally went back herself, she did not even look for Miles, but went straight to her own room. She saw that already Flora's things had been removed. That night when she went to bed, Miles came into her room and sat in silence in a chair there.

Comment

The most telling aspect to the chapter is Mrs. Grose's comment that she sees nothing across the lake. This seems to be a definite and direct statement by the author, but James who has balanced everything so carefully does not allow Mrs. Grose's statement to stand by itself. See the summary of the next chapter.

THE TURN OF THE SCREW

TEXTUAL ANALYSIS

CHAPTER XXI

Before daybreak of the next morning, Mrs. Grose came to the governess's room with the news that Flora was ill and feverish and had passed a night of unrest. Mrs. Grose told her companion that the child persisted in denying that she had ever seen anything and that every three minutes she would ask if the governess were coming. She did not, however, mention Miss Jessel at all. The governess replied that she could do nothing now except allow the children to play out their plot. The governess was sure that Flora wanted to make her, the governess, out to be the lowest kind of creature before the uncle. Without any such indication from Mrs. Grose, the governess continued with the idea that she knew the servant had come to tell her to leave; instead, she commented, the servant should leave with Flora and leave her alone with Miles. Mrs. Grose should take the child to her uncle immediately, the governess said, for she felt that Miles wanted to give her a new chance, especially since he had come into her room to sit with her.

Mrs. Grose then told the governess that she would leave that morning with the girl because, although she had seen nothing the previous day, she had heard a great deal from the child, horrible things, during the night. The governess was grateful and felt that she had been justified in finding Mrs. Grose on her side. The child had said shocking things about the governess, and these had upset the servant. Mrs. Grose said, "I believe."

The governess felt joy to have a companion, but she remembered that her letter would get to town before Mrs. Grose and Flora. Mrs. Grose said that was not so, for although the letter was gone, she had learned from Luke that he had not taken it into town. The governess knew that Miles had taken the letter, but Mrs. Grose felt that this showed that Miles must have been stealing letters at school.

The governess made small of the letter and entreated Mrs. Grose to leave her alone with the boy. She was sure that she could save him. Mrs. Grose left with a vow that she herself would save the governess even without the saving of Miles.

Comment

To the governess, and to the reader, incidentally, it is a very important moment in her story when the modest and loyal housekeeper tells that she now believes what the governess has been saying. Of course, the reader cannot help but wonder what the things that little Flora has said could be. When within a few pages the governess finds that Miles claims his dismissal from school came about because of things he had said to the companions he liked in school, the only conclusion that one can draw is that the two children have learned special, adult words and things from their association with Peter Quint and Miss Jessel. At any rate, the chapter also sets the scene for the final meeting between the governess and Mills.

THE TURN OF THE SCREW

TEXTUAL ANALYSIS

CHAPTER XXII

....

As soon as she was sure that Flora and Mrs. Grose had left in the carriage, the governess felt some deep apprehension. She could see that the other servants were puzzled about what was actually taking place, but she felt that she was now master and that she must take command of the situation. One person who seemed not concerned was Miles, who, the governess found, had breakfast with his sister and then gone off by himself. The governess had decided to give him his freedom until the proper time.

Then the two sat down to dinner. Finally Miles asked if his sister were really ill. The governess replied that she would be better in London because Bly ceased to agree with her. Miles wanted to know why his sister had not been sent before if her illness were not sudden. The governess replied this time that the journey would help the girl.

Miles was quite for some time. He got up from the table, looked out the window, and after a servant had cleared the table he turned and said, "Well-so we're alone!"

THE TURN OF THE SCREW

TEXTUAL ANALYSIS

CHAPTER XXIII

....

The governess took up Miles's last remark that they were now alone and said that they were not "absolutely" alone. (She is referring to the ghosts.) Miles went to the window. The governess thought that they were near the truth. Miles then said that he liked Bly and had felt much freedom the last twenty-four hours. The governess assured the boy that she stayed on only to allow him to enjoy his freedom, but shortly she confessed that she wanted to help him, as she had told him before, and had stayed on because she expected Miles to tell her "something".

The boy wanted to know if she meant she wanted to hear that "something" now. The governess felt there was no better time. She knew, as she recorded it in the manuscript, that the two were circling around like fighters. Then Miles said that he could not say anything right at that time because he had to see Luke. Before she allowed him to go, however, the governess said that she wanted a "smaller request" of him. She asked him directly if he had taken her letter to the uncle from the table yesterday.

THE TURN OF THE SCREW

TEXTUAL ANALYSIS

CHAPTER XXIV

Before she had a chance to note what Miles's reaction would be to what she had just said, the governess felt in an instant a presence. She had time only to hold the boy. At the window she saw Peter Quint, "his white face of damnation" pervading the room. She felt that her duty was to keep the boy unaware at the time. "It was like fighting with a demon for a human soul."

The boy admitted that he had taken the letter. He said he had taken it to see what she had said about him. He had opened the letter, but, he agreed with her, he had found nothing. The governess kissed him, and he told her he had burned the letter. Then she asked him if that was what he had done at school. Miles was surprised that she knew everything, but he said that he did not steal at school. She asked him what he did. He answered that he "said things" to the people he liked and that they probably repeated the things to the people they liked until those very things got around to the masters at the school. She pressed him to know exactly what he had said.

At this point, fully aware of the face at the window, the governess suddenly held the boy. She shrieked until Miles asked her if she was there. The governess was so surprised to hear "she" that she echoed the word back, and he said, "Miss Jessel, Miss Jessel," into her face. The governess said she seized the chance and wanted only to show the boy the face. She said it was not Miss Jessel, it was at the window. The boy looked around, bewildered, missing wholly the place where the face was. He asked, "It's he?" The governess pressed her chance with a question, "Whom do you mean by 'he'?" Miles turned around the room. "Peter Quint-you devil!" he said. "Where?" The governess considered this a "supreme surrender," and she tried to show Miles where the man was. But Miles "uttered the cry of a creature hurled over an abyss" and fell. The governess caught him, but she knew that he had died. "We were alone with the quiet day, and his little heart, dispossessed, had stopped."

Comment

There is no question that the governess forces to a crisis this climactic and shocking final scene in the story. It is the moment that she must bring about. The moment that she has with fear, but also with courage, been waiting for since the time that she decided the children were lost and that she must save them. One can say that Flora has been lost completely, this is the governess's final opportunity.

As soon as she knows or senses the presence of Peter Quint, the governess says that she is fighting a demon for a human soul. From the point of view of the governess that is exactly what the story has been about: she is fighting to free the soul of Miles. The only way that this is possible, she has decided, is to make the boy confess and reject finally the evil presence of Quint. She feels triumphant when she forces Miles to speak the name of Quint and when the boy refers to the ghost as "you devil." That Miles must die can also be understood in this context: although the governess is freeing him, the boy has been corrupted by the evil influence of the former servant. It is a case where evil and innocence reside together, not separately.

Of course, perfectly in keeping with the pattern of the story, the evidence of Miles's not seeing the ghost speaks out strongly against the design of the governess. The reader can note that all of the last chapter can be read in quite a different manner from that above. If Miles does not see the ghost, if his "devil" is really the governess, if he truly thinks up to this point that only Miss Jessel is haunting the governess - he would have heard that for the first time from his sister in the morning before she left with Mrs. Grose - then the governess has violated the innocence of the boy, forced on him her deranged mind, and killed him. In any way that one approaches the story, so long as he brings his own imagination, as James says he must, the tale is truly a shocking horror story.

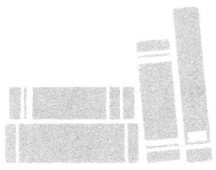

THE TURN OF THE SCREW

CHARACTER ANALYSES

Note: It is obvious from a reading of the story that, however ambiguous, there is actually only one character fully and completely developed. That character is the narrator of the tale, the governess. The other figures in the novel are actually what her description, her mind, her imagination make of them. *The Turn of the Screw*, therefore, is a matter of the governess, and the following character sketches take that fact into account.

THE GOVERNESS

The unnamed governess, who at twenty years of age goes to London to secure a position, fills her role in the story well, for as a narrator she is very personal, emotionally involved, almost high strung, but she is very complete in telling her story so that what struck her is made clear, but extraneous matters, those things that might make the subject of another story that is not hers, she leaves out completely. Before one turns to her involvement, however, one learns in the introductory, prologue-like chapter some important information. She is the youngest daughter of a country parson, fully, perhaps painfully aware, of her position and need to secure for the first time a job in the "service of the classroom," as the English call it. She is immediately overcome by the handsome bachelor who interviews her: he is a figure in the prime of his life and one that an anxious young girl would find in her dreams or in old novels. The image of this man sustains her through her ordeal; she feels that she has been rewarded by meeting him; his wealth, his looks, his home greatly impress her. These are the background facts that Douglas, the man who has the manuscript and who gives it to the author of the tale, gives about the governess. But he also adds that she was a charming lady, whom he liked extremely when she cared for his sister.

The governess's own words give more of the picture that one finally has of her. She is a young lady capable of deep emotion as one finds when she is confronted by the ghosts. She responds in shrieks sometimes, in exclamations, but always physically. Her language is exciting, just as she is. Yet she is capable of very great subtlety. She is constantly interpreting; she is constantly on guard to catch special meanings in what Mrs. Grose, Miles, and Flora say to her. The reader feels her going to the heights of exhilaration as she caresses the children, or when she hugs and kisses them, or the reader feels the depths of despair and horror as she is confronted by the ghosts. She is, therefore, a young schoolmistress, an impressionable, emotional, excitable, but intelligent, perceptive, sincere, and open girl. In other words, if one sympathizes with her, there is ample evidence that she deserves sympathy; if one suspects her, suspicion can be justified also.

It is this ambiguity that is so difficult to apprehend, but that is also what is so complete in her portrait as Henry James presents it. On the basis of the evidence that the governess gives the reader must decide whether or not the ghosts actually exist. The answer to that is the answer to the way one reads *The Turn of the Screw* and characterizes the governess. If one decides that the ghosts really do exist - and it seems from Henry James's preface to the work that he intended them to be part of the real world - then the governess is a woman of innocence, eager to walk into a world in which she has her position, where she is "at the helm." She commits herself to the children, ideally as a way to satisfy her vision of being associated with the beautiful master, the uncle. When she sees the ghosts, she realizes that they pervade the life of the children with evil. The governess is caught in the struggle to save the children and free them of the evil embodiments in their past association with Peter Quint and Miss Jessel. That then is the quest of the governess, who moves from the innocent position of schoolteacher to the complicated and experienced world of morality in the face of evil.

Although one cannot go so far as to say that the governess emerges as a noble figure, one must at least admire the resolute decision she makes to save the children. That she ultimately loses does not reflect on her character, but on the problem of how evil and innocence reside in the world. The governess, when one believes, is the innocent person reacting to the world of experience.

If the ghosts are hallucinations, figments of a young inexperienced dreamer's mind, then the consequences are significantly more dire. Then with her active imagination, her need for love, her infatuation over the handsome uncle, her personal repressions so well manifested in her impulsive hugging and kissing of the children, and the innuendoes of her thoughts about Miles - the governess is the corrupter of the innocent young children. This is a harsh judgment, but the governess's life of appearances, and of her taking things by their outward look, is a violation of the world of reality. To satisfy herself, she must convince the innocent children and the innocent Mrs. Grose. When she exposes them all to the presence of evil and forces them to accept it, she causes the deep illness of Flora, the divorce from the affections of the children of Mrs. Grose, and the death of Miles. She is, therefore, a dangerous corrupter, a demented, frustrated woman.

These two aspects, or contrasts, possible in the character of the governess are the extremes. As all the criticism of the novel indicates, it will not do to say that the governess is both one thing and another. Every reader must decide the basic question - are there ghosts, or not? - and then be willing to carry out the character sketch of the governess. From the purely esthetic point of view, the reader can see Henry James has explored in this story the limits of **realism**, both external and internal, and presented a portrait that can satisfy only when the reader allows his own experience, his own feelings, to act and decide.

MRS. GROSE

The illiterate, but very sympathetic, housekeeper and servant (and companion) to the children has a minor place in the story, but she is very important. Mrs. Grose is loyal to the children and her position. She strikes a realistic note throughout the work. Although she does not see the ghosts, she allows the governess to go on in her beliefs. As she says, she was willing to do so because she wanted to know herself. When she hears the words of the ill Flora - the reader wonders what the child could have said, just as the reader wonders about so many unsaid things in the story - Mrs. Grose believes the governess and realizes that the final drastic move of going to the distant uncle, surely an extreme move for the humble servant, must be made. Mrs. Grose concludes that Miles must have stolen at school, and she considers that a very terrible thing. Finally, it is Mrs. Grose who recognizes the portraits of Miss Jessel and Peter Quint. She had not approved of their behavior. All of these facts show that the servant has a special place in the story; the note of **realism** that she sounds is very important in order to understand the direction that the interpretations of the governess will take.

MILES

The precocious ten-year-old boy, who has committed some unnamed wrong at school by the things that he has said to the boys he liked there, is either evil or a young lad who by the end of the novel has been corrupted by the neurotic governess. When one says that Miles is evil, he means that Peter Quint, in his being constantly with the boy in the past, has brought the boy to the world of experience beyond what a boy of Miles's age should know. It means that Quint, in his insinuating way, has taught the boy the things he said at school and has caused him to seek the evil that the older man represents. Of course, this is exactly the way that the governess interprets the behavior of Miles. On the other hand, one can say that Miles's going out at night and blowing out the candle are simply boyish pranks of a young boy who finds himself constantly watched by an overly-attentive governess. Even Miles's "said things" at school might be the repetition of the men's talk he might have heard from Peter Quint. Finally, although the governess interprets everything that little Miles says in her presence, he might be doing nothing more than speaking quite directly. In the last chapter, the reader finds it hard to understand if Miles does actually see Peter Quint, or what the import of the boy's calling out "devil" with Quint's name might be. Either Quint has won in his pursuit of Miles - therefore, the boy has succumbed to evil - or the governess has killed an innocent child.

FLORA

The eight-year-old sister of Miles is less completely involved in the manuscript of the governess than her brother. She, too, may be an innocent child who plays along in her brother's little games on the governess. She is bright, and like her brother, beautiful. She is completely upset by the governess's open mention of Miss Jessel. The reader can at least sense what the relationship between Quint and Miles might have been, but Flora seems only a companion to Miss Jessel as she accompanies Peter Quint. Yet, it is this implied relationship that gives the reader the material to infer that Flora, like her brother, has fallen from innocence and is now sought by the female demon in the story. The child is precocious, but she succumbs to the pervasive influence and atmosphere of evil in the story.

PETER QUINT

Most of the information about Peter Quint comes from Mrs. Grose and perhaps from the townspeople to whom the governess has spoken. What little we know of the former servant is interesting. He assumed his position, he became overfriendly with Miles, and he emulated the master in dress. Mrs. Grose says that they were aware that the clothes were missing. He was a very handsome man, but immediately the governess knows that he is not a gentleman. If he is evil - and any decision on the ghosts would make him that - and a devil, certainly, his red hair is an extension of that picture metaphorically. The air of corruption that surrounds Peter Quint is further emphasized by the governess learning that he was found dead on the road from the village from a blow on the head. Of course, all this is on the evidence in the story, for Quint, even as a ghost, does not act. He only appears, but it is he who causes the action of the story.

MISS JESSEL

The former governess has come to a sad end: she has left and died after having a relationship with Peter Quint. Mrs. Grose hints very strongly that it was that very relationship that she found so objectionable, especially since she would see the children taken along with the older lovers. Each time the governess sees her predecessor, her descriptions are always in terms of a lost and bereaved woman, a woman of guilt who has suffered tragedy. Miss Jessel, like Flora, whom she may have led astray, is given a lesser role than her male counterpart.

THE UNCLE

This man, who so affects the governess, resides in the background of the story but his presence is very strong. First, one must realize that he causes the young governess to accept his condition that she take over the care of the children and not bother him because he has his personal matters to care for. Then, one realizes that the other characters in the work always think of him, or getting in touch with him, as the ultimate step. Mrs. Grose was reluctant to do that in the past, and the governess, because of her fears of proving inadequate, feels the same way in the present. Of course, the governess idealizes him, but one wonders if the rich bachelor gentleman in his impressive home is really not a picture of a dream for a country parson's twenty-year-old daughter.

DOUGLAS

Although the owner of the manuscript of the governess seems to be in the introductory chapter just to get the story underway, one senses that he has a deeper involvement in the actual story itself, if for no other reason than for his acquaintance with the governess. Douglas feels it is necessary to give the necessary background to the story. Although he knows the tale, he clearly states that the governess was a charming lady and that he liked her very much even if she was ten years older than he. Of course, that would mean that he sees the following story exactly from the point of view of the governess. If for no other reason Douglas could be considered an important character, that would be reason enough.

THE NARRATOR

Although the tale is told by the governess, one can note that the author tells the reader that he heard, with a group of friends, the story from Douglas. The narrator of the first chapter was sufficiently interested in the story so that Douglas bequeathed the manuscript to him.

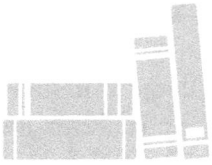

THE TURN OF THE SCREW

TEXTUAL ANALYSIS

CHAPTER XXIV

Before she had a chance to note what Miles's reaction would be to what she had just said, the governess felt in an instant a presence. She had time only to hold the boy. At the window she saw Peter Quint, "his white face of damnation" pervading the room. She felt that her duty was to keep the boy unaware at the time. "It was like fighting with a demon for a human soul."

The boy admitted that he had taken the letter. He said he had taken it to see what she had said about him. He had opened the letter, but, he agreed with her, he had found nothing. The governess kissed him, and he told her he had burned the letter. Then she asked him if that was what he had done at school. Miles was surprised that she knew everything, but he said that he did not steal at school. She asked him what he did. He answered that he "said things" to the people he liked and that they probably repeated the things to the people they liked until those very things got around to the masters at the school. She pressed him to know exactly what he had said.

At this point, fully aware of the face at the window, the governess suddenly held the boy. She shrieked until Miles asked her if she was there. The governess was so surprised to hear "she" that she echoed the word back, and he said, "Miss Jessel, Miss Jessel," into her face. The governess said she seized the chance and wanted only to show the boy the face. She said it was not Miss Jessel, it was at the window. The boy looked around, bewildered, missing wholly the place where the face was. He asked, "It's he?" The governess pressed her chance with a question, "Whom do you mean by 'he'?" Miles turned around the room. "Peter Quint-you devil!" he said. "Where?" The governess considered this a "supreme surrender," and she tried to show Miles where the man was. But Miles "uttered the cry of a creature hurled over an abyss" and fell. The governess caught him, but she knew that he had died. "We were alone with the quiet day, and his little heart, dispossessed, had stopped."

Comment

There is no question that the governess forces to a crisis this climactic and shocking final scene in the story. It is the moment that she must bring about. The moment that she has with fear, but also with courage, been waiting for since the time that she decided the children were lost and that she must save them. One can say that Flora has been lost completely, this is the governess's final opportunity.

As soon as she knows or senses the presence of Peter Quint, the governess says that she is fighting a demon for a human soul. From the point of view of the governess that is exactly what the story has been about: she is fighting to free the soul of Miles. The only way that this is possible, she has decided, is to make the boy confess and reject finally the evil presence of Quint. She feels triumphant when she forces Miles to speak the name of Quint and when the boy refers to the ghost as "you devil." That Miles must die can also be understood in this context: although the governess is freeing him, the boy has been corrupted by the evil influence of the former servant. It is a case where evil and innocence reside together, not separately.

Of course, perfectly in keeping with the pattern of the story, the evidence of Miles's not seeing the ghost speaks out strongly against the design of the governess. The reader can note that all of the last chapter can be read in quite a different manner from that above. If Miles does not see the ghost, if his "devil" is really the governess, if he truly thinks up to this point that only Miss Jessel is haunting the governess - he would have heard that for the first time from his sister in the morning before she left with Mrs. Grose - then the governess has violated the innocence of the boy, forced on him her deranged mind, and killed him. In any way that one approaches the story, so long as he brings his own imagination, as James says he must, the tale is truly a shocking horror story.

THE TURN OF THE SCREW

CRITICAL COMMENTARY

HENRY JAMES' OWN PREFACE

Between 1907 and 1917 there appeared a collected edition of the works of Henry James issued by Charles Scribner's. This edition is always referred to as The New York Edition. To each one of the volumes in the collection, James wrote a "preface" in which he usually detailed the way he came upon the story of the work, the special problems he encountered, and the way he handled these. *The Turn of the Screw* appeared in the same volume with two other works: *The Aspern Papers* and *The Liar*. In the section of the preface where James discusses *The Turn of the Screw*, he makes some important comments that can be very useful for a student who wants to decide on what may be the proper interpretation for this complicated and subtle story. Of course, the student should consult the other works, for critics have disagreed with James himself on exactly what kind of work he wrote (as opposed to the kind of work he thought he wrote).

James refers to *The Turn of the Screw* as a "perfectly independent and irresponsible little fiction." He also says that this particular work is least likely to be the subject of "earnest criticism." He is quite wrong on that point. James then reveals how the story came to him in the first place: on a winter afternoon in an old country-house, the conversation turned to the problem of apparitions and night-fears. The more modern "psychical" stories seemed no longer to satisfy people. As the group was lamenting the loss of a good type of story, the host said that he regretted that he could not put together a story that he had heard when he was younger. The story had to do with a woman in charge of children and some certain "bad" spirits, of servants dead, who were trying to get hold of the children. That was all that he heard, James says. But that was what he himself referred to as a "germ" of a story. When he was asked to do a story for a magazine, he says, he thought of this "sinister romance."

What he liked about the possibilities in this "fairy-tale pure and simple" was the chance he had of giving his imagination free rein. The hard part was to improvise with the story and still keep within the bounds that it provided. The whole idea was to complicate the mystification of his "friend," the "superstitious narrator."

The ghosts were another problem, says James. Good ghosts, he says, do nothing. He wanted his ghosts to cause the whole situation "to reek with the air of Evil." Peter Quint and Miss Jessel are not really ghosts, he continues, but he wanted them to be like "demons as loosely constructed as those of the old trials for witchcraft." In other words, he wanted ghosts that would cause the children to act, or ghosts that would woo their victims. He says that the essence of the whole story was how these predatory creatures caused their villainy to be felt on the children. He was looking to pervade the story with hints of their evil.

Finally, James concluded, only by making the reader's vision of evil so great and causing him to reflect with his own imagination, with his own sympathy for the children, and especially with his horror of the demons could the whole sense of the story be accomplished. James feels he does not need the specifics if he can make the reader feel or think the evil.

EDMUND WILSON, THE AMBIGUITY OF HENRY JAMES, IN THE TRIPLE THINKERS

This long study of the ambiguity in the works of Henry James begins with a study of *The Turn of the Screw*, probably the most famous discussion of a particular point of view of the work. Wilson, a famous critic, says that this story conceals quite another horror tale under its obvious, literal one. His theory, quite directly stated by the author, is that the governess, who is telling her own story, is really suffering from a neurotic case of sex repression and that the ghosts do not really exist in the work but are simply hallucinations from which she suffers. Wilson then traces the story very closely, and some of his comments are as follows: He points out that the governess looks for work and she is completely infatuated by the uncle. When she gets the letter from the headmaster of Mile's school without adequate evidence she decides that there is something ominous in the background. As the governess wanders around the estate, she is constantly thinking about the uncle and wanting to see him. When she sees Peter Quint, she convinces herself that he has returned to haunt the children. Then the governess sees the figure of Miss Jessel as Flora is playing with the little pieces of wood. (Wilson will make much of these pieces of wood.)

Wilson says that there is no evidence to show that anyone else beside the governess sees the ghost's. The servant does not see them. The children become hysterical when the governess tries to force them to see them. Wilson says that there is a

Freudian significance to the governess seeing a ghost when she sees a child trying to fit a piece of wood in a hole in another piece, or when the governess sees a man on a tower. Wilson in the original essay cannot explain how the governess can described Quint's appearance so well (see below), but he asks if this cannot be a matter of the governess's subconscious imagination and a matter of confusion with the master, the uncle, that is.

Wilson reviews the confrontations with the ghosts. He examines particularly the ending of the story and shows that Miles does not see the ghost. He says that the governess literally frightens Miles to death.

Wilson says that once the reader sees that story in this way, he wonders how he could have read the story in any other way. The critic does admit that at no point does James give the whole story away. That the story can be read in two ways. Wilson is sure that his reading is right and points out that *The Turn of the Screw* was not included with the ghost stories in The New York Edition but with two stories that had obsessed narrators. Wilson says that this points out that *The Turn of the Screw* is primarily a characterization of the governess. If one thinks of her, one cannot help admit that as she is a poor parson's daughter, she is unable to admit her sexual impulses because of her background. Wilson also points out that there is a peculiar psychology to governesses. They are likely to become ingrown and morbid because of their position in the family. From this point on, Wilson goes on the discuss the entire development of Henry James and his complexity.

Wilson wrote his essay first in 1934, but he added to it substantially in 1948. Basically, he felt justified in his view. In 1959, he added a short further note on *The Turn of the Screw* (See Selected Bibliography), in which he made an explanation of the fact that the governess was so accurate in her description of Quint though she had not seen him. Wilson concludes that she must have received the information from the townspeople. He says there is evidence that she has spoken to them, and it is probably from them that she knows of the way Quint died.

A. J. A. WALDOCK ON MR. EDMUND WILSON AND THE TURN OF THE SCREW

This brief piece comes right to the point and states that Edmund Wilson's essay, its main point that the governess is a frustrated spinster, is untenable. The governess sees the apparition twice and then she reports to Mrs. Grose, says Waldock. The author points out two important aspects of the description. First, Mrs. Grose recognizes Quint positively, Second, up to that point the governess had never heard the name of Quint before. Waldock takes Wilson to task on these two points and says that Wilson's comment that almost everything in the work can be read with double meanings does not stand up if even one fact can be proved in the governess's story. Waldock asserts that there could not be confusion between Quint and the uncle. He says that even if one were to think that the governess were neurotic, etc., the fact of the matter is that any explanation would end up with the admission that she really did see ghosts. (See Bibliography for place where this essay can be found.)

CHARLES G. HOFFMAN ON INNOCENCE AND EVIL IN JAMES'S THE TURN OF THE SCREW

Hoffman points out that although James usually deals with the problem of social conflict, in this work he is concerned with the problem of innocence and evil, more specifically, the coexistence of innocence and evil as "evil-in-good." The author begins by explaining that it is significant that James chose, as his central characters in the drama of moral evil, the children. The choice of the governess as the point of view and the narrator is also significant, says Hoffman. It is through her point of view that the evil is revealed. The introductory section of the novel is designed to establish the point of view of the governess. The governess, however, has been the subject of controversy, especially in the elaboration of the Freudian theory of Edmund Wilson. Hoffman sees nothing particularly wrong in the youngest daughter of a country parson to be so infatuated by a gentleman, such as the uncle. Douglas in the introductory section, moreover, describes her as a "most charming person."

The narrative, Hoffman continues, begins quietly. All the details set the atmosphere. The reader gets the picture of an impressionable young lady. She is intense and perceptive in her impressions. The governess is somewhat disappointed that there is nothing special in Bly: there is no premonition of evil. It is this normal atmosphere that contrasts with the evil that will be built up. The first suggestion of something wrong is the letter about Miles. Mrs. Grose dismisses the whole thing, and the problem is not made definite. The problem of the governess's predecessor is also ambiguous. It is in the third chapter that the first note of evil is struck, that is, with the appearance of the ghost of Quint. In the next chapter, the governess is not sure about the ghost, but the second appearance shows that a simple explanation will not do.

The role of Mrs. Grose is important. She is realistic and a reminder of the actual world. Eventually, she believes in the ghosts although she does not see them. It is Mrs. Grose who recognizes the description of Quint in chapter five. Hoffman insists that the ghosts did appear and cites Henry James himself for proof. According to James's preface the figures of Quint and Miss Jessel are not stage ghosts with white sheets and clanging chains. They are ghosts that embody evil, they cause an atmosphere of evil. James concentrated on the effect the ghosts had on the characters in the work. This is James's success in the work.

Hoffman then proceeds to show how the involvement of the children delineates the innocence and evil **theme**. The children at first are in the background. Through images, beauty and light for innocence, ugliness and darkness for evil, James presents his contrasts. Miles is beautiful and brilliant, directly in contrast to the dusk which surrounds him. But in Miles, there is also darkness, for example, in the questions that he raises. The same balance resides in Flora. The governess gets a psychological shock when she sees the transformation from light and innocence to darkness and evil in Flora after the last appearance of Miss Jessel. At that point Miss Jessel has won (Chapters XIX and XX) and Flora has turned to evil.

The governess then tries to save Miles. He must confess if he is to be saved, for one realizes that though he is beautiful, there is evil in him as evidenced by the dismissal from school. Quint and Miss Jessel are agents of evil, not evil itself; they draw out evil that already resides in the children. It is ironic that the governess, who is not evil, is a figure who also draws out the evil in the children. Flora is finally lost because the governess forces her evil to be revealed. In the case of Miles, it is his confession (that he stole the letter) which causes the ghost of Quint to appear. Miles acknowledges the ghost, says Hoffman. At that point, Miles had confessed, Quint has lost, the governess has saved Miles. The recognition and the horror of the evil, however, kill the boy.

The final problem of whether good and evil exist outside the individual is never answered in the story. It is left ambiguous. Evil coexists with good, so far as the novel presents its case. The governess learns this lesson in the final scene, when Miles admits the existence of Peter Quint.

Note: There are many other articles on *The Turn of the Screw* but the ones here discussed cover the major areas that are usually considered. They contain the central problems that all readers must confront. All the works cited in the Selected Bibliography have studies of this work. Students can begin there, especially with the edition of Gerald Willen, which contains all the necessary information for a complete reading.

THE TURN OF THE SCREW

ESSAY QUESTIONS AND ANSWERS

Question: A successful Broadway play with the title "The Innocents" was adapted from *The Turn of the Screw*. Discuss the appropriateness of that title.

Answer: In *The Turn of the Screw* Henry James has chosen as central figures two children. They are described as being beautiful and on first appearance they seem to be innocent, innocent in the sense that they have not been exposed to the sin and evil in the world. No matter how one interprets the tale, whether it be from the point of view of the governess who tells, the story or from the view of an analysis of psychological disorder, one must understand that the children have been corrupted before the appearance of the governess by Peter Quint and Miss Jessel, or are in the process of their innocence's disappearing in the tale itself. The dark hints of Mrs. Grose that Quint was always with Miles and that the boy followed the older man around coupled with the fact that the young boy has been dismissed from school, seem to indicate that the boy is no longer innocent. Either knowingly or not, he is the agent of corruption. The same holds true of Flora's precocious responses to the governess and her willingness to participate in her brother's deceits. Of course, one can add the dimension of the governess's involvement in the tale. If the children are innocent, then it is she who shows them that their pure world is now surrounded by evil. When one thinks of Flora and Miles as innocent beings, he realizes that the entire story becomes one of the struggle between good and evil. Therefore, the title, "The Innocents," is particularly appropriate.

Question: Discuss the possibilities of meanings in interpretation, or the ambiguities that exist in the story.

Answer: Much of the criticism of *The Turn of the Screw* has taken cognizance, sometimes with dismay, that almost everything in the story can be taken two ways. When the reader thinks that one particular interpretation is the only and proper one, he realizes on closer examination that Henry James has never really tipped his hand. In other words, his shuffle is constantly turning up new tricks. Therefore, the story is ultimately ambiguous.

The basic question that one must ask is the following: do the ghosts really exist in the story, or are they simply in the imagination of the governess. If the ghosts do exist - and there seems to be much evidence in the clarity with which the governess reports them, the reactions of Mrs. Grose, and the effects on the children - then the governess is perfectly sane and almost a noble figure. Once she knows the ghosts exist, she decides that she must save the children from their pursuit.

The governess becomes a figure who champions the children and tries to save them from the evil and corruption that the figures of Peter Quint and Miss Jessel are trying to perpetuate. If the ghosts do not exist except in the mind of the governess - the reader can note that no one else actually sees the figures, that the governess forces her interpretations on others, and that they appear only when the governess is daydreaming or in imagined crisis - then the governess is a neurotic person who takes over a new position and forces the children to recognize evil for the first time. It would seem from the evidence of the story that Henry James meant the first of these possibilities as the subject of his story. On the other hand, it may be completely possible that he built into his tale the second and contrary aspect without ever realizing it.

Question: Explain the meanings of the ghosts as the governess interprets them.

Answer: When the governess first sees the ghost of Peter Quint on the tower of Bly, she has been thinking about the children's uncle. Specifically, she has been thinking that she would like to see the handsome bachelor from the impressive house on Harley Street in London. It would seem that she confuses the former servant with a man of her dreams. After she has seen Quint a second time, she is able to describe him in almost too accurate detail. It is this second time that causes her to decide that the ghost is not after her, but Miles. That decision colors much of her thinking about Quint. With the information from Mrs. Grose, the governess decides that Quint is evil and has been the corrupter of Miles. She sees him as a direct threat on the children and therefore on herself. In other words, Quint is a demon who is trying to claim the child through his evil.

The governess always sees her predecessor, Miss Jessel, as a lost and wretched woman. Again, from what she has heard from Mrs. Grose, the governess assumes that Miss Jessel has fallen to a lower-class man in Quint. One can only conjecture on what she thinks the actual relationship between the two must have been. Mrs. Grose hints strongly that Miss Jessel had to leave Bly because of that relationship. In other words, Miss Jessel, too, is evil and lost. She is a wretched creature, just as persistent in her desire to draw the children to her, even as she appears in an attitude of woe.

Together, the ghosts are demons that cause the others to act. They force the crises in the novel, the second of which kills the young Miles. They are to the governess figures that cause dread and horror. The effect of *The Turn of the Screw* on the reader depends on what the presence of these mean to that reader.

Question: Discuss the significance of the minor figures in the story and how they affect interpretation.

Answer: There are four minor figures that any reading of the novel should take into consideration. First, there is the modest, humble, and loyal housekeeper, Mrs. Grose. Much of the information that the governess has comes from her constant questions of Mrs. Grose. It is the servant who recognizes the description of Quint and tells the governess what kind of man he was. Mrs. Grose did not approve of the way the dead man behaved with Miles and other people; also, she did not approve of a lady's taking up with a lower-class man, as Miss Jessel obviously did. Mrs. Grose affects the interpretation of the story in two very important places. In the shocking scene beside the lake, when the governess brings up the name of Miss Jessel to the frightened Flora, Mrs. Grose does not see the ghost. The next day, however, tells the governess that she now believes the things she has been saying. The reader must take these into consideration, for Mrs. Grose strikes a simple, realistic tone in the novel.

Another minor figure, who does not affect the reading of the story, but who lurks in the background of the tale and in the mind of the governess, is the uncle of the children. His distance, his order that he not be bothered, and the fear with which his name is invoked by the governess and Mrs. Grose add a further dimension to the horror tale.

Two figures from the introductory chapter are interesting to note. The more important is the man Douglas, who reads the manuscript. He also provides the background of the governess and informs the gathering that he thought her a pleasant woman and that he liked her very much. These statements cannot help but influence the reader's attitude towards the governess. The man who is writing the story, the author and narrator of the introductory chapter, shows deep interest in the tale he is to hear from Douglas. Although he does sense some humor, he is sure that the story is one of dread, horror, and importance. One can call this last character Henry James himself.

DAISY MILLER

INTRODUCTION

INTRODUCTION

"*Daisy Miller*: A Study" first appeared in *Cornhill Magazine* in England in 1878 and came out in book form the following year. This publication occurred after an American publisher had rejected it. The story was an immediate success and projected James into fame for the first time. At first, the character of Daisy was considered an "outrage." Subsequently, that opinion changed. To many critics, this short novel is a full expression of James's most important **theme**: his international subject, or the confrontation between a youthful, innocent girl and a Europeanized society that has played out its ideas and is now living in the **conventions** and formalities of a structured society. Daisy Miller is in a direct line with the best of James's female creations caught in this very same problem. There is no question that Daisy looks forward to Isabel Archer in *The Portrait of a Lady* and Milly Theale in *The Wings of the Dove*. Daisy is a much clearer, more idealized version of these later heroines, but this short work contains all of James's essential thoughts on the international theme.

Daisy Miller has with *The Turn of the Screw* remained one of James's most popular works. It may well be that the success of the work lies in the fact that James hit on what is essentially still a popular type story today. Much modern literature is built on the situation of the holiday of pleasure that suddenly, shockingly, turns into a much more significant examination of life and its meanings. That is what James does with the young and beautiful Daisy. In the beginning she is a tourist. She is a certain type figure, but her personal drama turns into the classic life-death struggle. Basically, the story of Daisy is the subject of comedy, but it is important comedy that ends in tragedy. *Daisy Miller* is an important work in the development of Henry James's career, but it is also an important work in itself.

BRIEF SUMMARY OF STORY

The town of Vevey, Switzerland, was a stopping place for many American tourists in the month of June. Winter, a twenty-seven-year-old American, had come there from Geneva to see his aunt, Mrs. Costello, who always seemed to have a headache. After calling at her rooms and finding her indisposed, Winterbourne had gone for a walk, returned, had breakfast, and was having coffee in the garden of a well-known hotel when a small boy of nine or ten came up to him and asked him for sugar. Winterbourne talked with the boy and found he was an American who did not like Europe. Shortly, the boy's sister approached; she was a pretty American girl, thought Winterbourne. He found that the girl and her brother were going to Italy for the winter. The girl at first did not say much to the gentleman, but by asking the boy, Winterbourne found that the young boy's name was Randolph Miller and his sister was Daisy. They were from Schenectady, New York. Randolph did not want to go on to Rome; he wanted to return to America, he emphatically repeated. Finally, Daisy began to speak volubly about her family. Winterbourne, who had been living in Europe since he was about Randolph's present age, found himself at turns charmed and puzzled by the innocent and enthusiastic, unaffected beautiful girl. He did wonder if she were a flirt.

Winterbourne found that Daisy wanted to visit the Castle of Chillon, a famous tourist sight. Winterbourne said that the two could go together, but Eugenio, who was a guide and servant with the Millers, disapproved of the idea that they should visit the castle unattended. Daisy then said that they could go some other time.

Winterbourne thought that he could get his aunt, Mrs. Costello, to meet the Americans, but he found that his aunt had seen them at the hotel and did not approve of them at all. She said, "They are very common. They are the sort of Americans that one does one's duty by not-not accepting." Mrs. Costello also thought that they were much too familiar with their courier, Eugenio, and that they had never seen a gentleman with good manners. Mrs. Costello was shocked that Daisy would be willing to visit the Castle of Chillon with her nephew on such short acquaintance. The older woman warned the young man that he did not know the ways of American women because he had not been in that country for a long time.

Winterbourne was embarrassed when he saw Daisy, especially when she referred to the aunt that Winterbourne was to have introduced her to. He fell back on his aunt's poor health as an excuse. They saw Daisy's mother, and Winterbourne was quite surprised by the ease with which Daisy introduced him to her. Daisy then announced to her mother that she and Winterbourne were going to row over to the Castle that evening.

Winterbourne was excited by the idea of rowing a young girl to the sight, but Eugenio came upon them and insisted firmly that they not go alone.

Two days later, Daisy and Winterbourne did go to the Castle. Winterbourne could not quite understand the bold statements of the young lady. Daisy finally said that she would stop teasing him if he would promise to come down to Rome in the winter. Winterbourne said that that would be easy because his aunt had taken an apartment in that city for the winter. That evening Winterbourne told his aunt that he had been with Daisy that day, and the aunt said that Winterbourne was only confirming what she already felt about the young girl.

Winterbourne arrived in Rome towards the end of January. He had heard from his aunt that Daisy was intimate with "some third-rate Italians." Mrs. Costello thought the Millers hopelessly vulgar, although Winterbourne said that they were innocents. He met the Millers at a Mrs. Walker's place. Daisy chided Winterbourne for not coming to see her and criticized him good-naturedly about his behavior at Vevey. She then told Mrs. Walker that she was coming to her party, but also asked her to do the favor of inviting a Mr. Giovanelli, one of Daisy's friends. Mrs. Walker hesitated, but then said she would invite him.

When they were leaving, Daisy told the others to go ahead and said that she was going for a walk with Giovanelli. Mrs. Walker told her that it was not right for her to walk alone with an Italian at that hour. Daisy assumed that Mrs. Walker meant that she should not walk alone to meet the man, so she asked Winterbourne to accompany her to her rendezvous. Winterbourne did accompany her, resolved not to let her go off alone with the Italian. When they finally found Giovanelli, Daisy continued walking with the two men at her side. Winterbourne thought that the man could not be a gentleman to meet a young girl in broad daylight on a crowded street corner in Rome. He said to himself also, "Nevertheless, a nice girl ought to know!" And he wondered whether Daisy were really a nice girl.

They continued walking for a quarter of an hour, when Winterbourne saw Mrs. Walker's carriage and the lady seated in it. Mrs. Walker beckoned to Winterbourne and told him that Daisy should not conduct herself in such a manner in public, for it was a shame. Mrs. Walker spoke to Daisy and asked her to get into the carriage, but the young lady said she would not. Winterbourne also told her that he thought she should get into the carriage, but Daisy thought otherwise and went off with Giovanelli. Mrs. Walker told Winterbourne that the girl had gone too far and her behavior was scandalous, but Winterbourne said that it was really a matter of Daisy's being uncultivated. Mrs. Walker disagreed. She was very upset.

Daisy arrived at Mrs. Walker's ball after the other guests, who all stopped talking and looked at her. Although she had planned not to greet Daisy and her escort, Mrs. Walker finally did, but only tepidly. Winterbourne asked Daisy not to flirt with Giovanelli, because the man's designs were different from hers. Daisy told him that at least Giovanelli never said rude things to her. When Daisy came to take leave at the end of the evening, Mrs. Walker deliberately snubbed her. Daisy turned pale, her face grave.

Then Winterbourne saw Daisy in many places around the city; always she was accompanied by Giovanelli. Mrs. Costello was sure that Daisy and the Italian were carrying on an intrigue and told Winterbourne that. Winterbourne spoke to Mrs. Miller, but that had no effect whatsoever. One night Winterbourne went to the Colosseum and saw there in the darkness Daisy and

Giovanelli. Winterbourne was horrified to see them there. He told Daisy that she should know that it was dangerous to be there in the summer because of Roman fever (that is, malaria). Giovanelli said that he had warned her, but she insisted on coming there.

Winterbourne mentioned to no one that he had seen Daisy at the Colosseum at midnight with Giovanelli. A day or two later, Winterbourne heard that Daisy was quite ill. He went to her place. There Mrs. Miller told him that Daisy wanted him to know that she was not engaged. A week later, Daisy died; she was buried in a small cemetery. At the ceremony, Winterbourne talked with Giovanelli, who said of Daisy, "She was the most innocent." He also told Winterbourne that Daisy would never have married him.

Winterbourne told Mrs. Costello that he had been unjust to Daisy. The message that she had sent to him before her death had shown that they had not understood the young lady. "She would have appreciated one's esteem," said Winterbourne. He realized that Daisy did after all want to be accepted. Winterbourne at the end returned to Geneva.

DETAILED SUMMARY WITH COMMENTS

Daisy Miller consists of two long parts without chapter breaks within each section. The following is a summary of each part. The summary follows the story very closely so that at significant points in it there are comments on what the reader should carefully note.

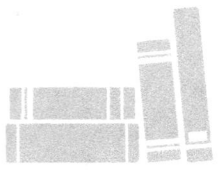

DAISY MILLER

TEXTUAL ANALYSIS

PART I

The little town of Vevey, Switzerland, had many hotels for the large tourist trade that came there. These hotels lined the shore of a remarkably blue lake, and among the newer places was a famous and classical stopping place, which in the month of June was full of numerous touring Americans. A person could see young American girls in the area, especially from an inn named the "Trois Couronnes." One could also see the mixture of German waiters, Russian princesses, and Polish boys.

One does not know if a young American sitting at the inn was thinking about these things on a beautiful summer morning two or three years ago. The American was a twenty-seven-year-old man named Winterbourne, who had come from Geneva the day before to visit his aunt staying at a hotel there. It was said about Winterbourne that he was "studying" in Geneva all these years. The truth was that he had gone to grammar school and college there, in the "little metropolis of Calvinism," but some said he had an attachment for an older woman there.

Comment

Winterbourne is the point of view from which the reader sees the story of the young American girl. That is to say, the story is presented as Winterbourne sees it and experiences it. One will note shortly that Daisy is seen and heard in the tale. Her point of view is never given. James many times referred to a character such as Winterbourne as his "central consciousness." That is perhaps a better term at this point, because much of the story and its meanings come out in the way that Winterbourne thinks and why he thinks as he does.

Already, James has presented a great deal of that information. Winterbourne has lived in Europe for a long time. He is in many ways a European, or at least, he is Europeanized. In all of James's works, this is a very special type of character, one who has lost the spontaneity of his American ways and has acquired the set ways of Europe. A small hint of this last statement is the fact that Winterbourne, with his frigid, symbolic name, likes the city of Calvin, the founder of a rigid and deterministic form of Protestantism that eventually became Puritanism.

Winterbourne had called at his aunt's but as usual she had a headache and could not see him. He had taken a walk, had breakfast, and was now having coffee. As he lit a cigarette, a diminutive boy of eight or nine came down the path with a long, pointed stick which he stabbed into everything. The boy asked Winterbourne if he had any sugar. Winterbourne showed him some lumps remaining on the table and the boy selected one and tried to bite it. He complained about his teeth and blamed it all on "this old Europe." He complained that he could not get American candy, which was the "best," in Europe. The boy was an American, and Winterbourne said he was too.

Comment

The precocious, independent, bold, young Randolph Miller is probably an American portrait. It is not a very attractive one, but it has a freshness to it. At any rate, the story takes a step forward in the little boy's complaining about "this old Europe." That is the subject of the story: Americans in Europe. The difficulty that Winterbourne has in understanding Randolph shows Winterbourne's loss of identity with the Americans.

The boy then said that his sister, who was always "blowing" at him, was coming. Winterbourne noticed a beautiful young lady, dressed in white muslin with many frills. She was bareheaded, carried a parasol, and was walking towards them. The girl admonished her brother, who was now using his stick for pole-vaulting. Winterbourne assumed that when Randolph referred to him as an American to the sister that that was a sort of introduction and tried to talk to the girl, fully aware all the time that he would not do so in Geneva unless he were properly introduced.

Comment

It is this type of thought that the story is built on, for the subject will always be what the Europeans think of a particular way of behaving. That Winterbourne assumes he can behave with Daisy in a way that differs from the way he knows he is supposed to behave with a European girl is interesting, as the reader will soon see. He is embarrassed, but he ventures to speak to her.

At first the young girl did not speak to the man, but Winterbourne ask her, when she mentioned it to her brother, if she were going to Italy. She glanced at him and said, "Yes, sir," and said no more. The girl struck Winterbourne as being not at all offended or perplexed by his speaking to her, so he became less and less embarrassed. Although she did not look at him directly when he spoke to her at first, he was not surprised because that must have been her manner. As he pointed out some of the interesting sights in view, she did look at him without shrinking. It was not a bold look, but an honest and fresh one, Winterbourne reflected. Always an admirer of feminine beauty, he observed that she was a beautiful girl. "He was sure she had a spirit of her own, but in her bright, sweet, superficial little visage there was no mockery, no irony." Winterbourne learned from the girl that she, her brother, and mother were on their way to Rome for the winter, but he learned more by getting Randolph to his side.

From Randolph, Winterbourne first learned his name. Then he found that the girl's name was "Daisy Miller" but her real name was Annie P. Miller. The father was a wealthy businessman in Schenectady, New York; his name, Ezra P. Miller. Winterbourne let the boy go, and Daisy commented that her little brother did not like Europe and wanted to return, "right home" to America. The two continued to converse about the family, and Winterbourne was quite pleased to hear a pretty young girl speak so much and volubly. Daisy gave a history of the family's movements in Europe. She complained in her open and honest manner that she had not seen any "society" yet, as she was accustomed to in New York. She wondered if any such thing existed. She explained that she had many gentlemen friends.

Winterbourne was "amused, perplexed, and decidedly charmed" by the talk of the young lady. He had never heard such open and frank talk from a girl. He did not know how this would be taken in Geneva. He was not sure if she were simply a pretty girl from New York State, or an audacious, unscrupulous person. He had been told that American girls were "exceedingly innocent," but some people had told him that they were not. Winterbourne thought that the girl was a "pretty flirt," "very unsophisticated." He did not know how one behaved with a flirt, but he was comfortable in his decision.

Comment

Already the character of Daisy and what she represents is before the reader. The difficulty later is that Winterbourne does not fully realize exactly what he has seen in the young girl. Daisy is of a completely open and honest nature. She is voluble, pleasant, refreshingly honest, direct, young, and enthusiastic. After these matters, however, she is completely and honestly innocent. She is innocent in a completely unsophisticated way. These are the most important aspects of her character. The reader should understand - and Henry James meant it that way - that Daisy cannot by nature be a calculating and designing person. Later in the story, this point must be kept in mind.

Of course, a special tone is struck with Winterbourne's decision that Daisy is a "flirt."

Daisy asked Winterbourne if he had ever been to the Chateau de Chillon (the setting for the famous poem by Lord Byron, "The Prisoner of Chillon"). Winterbourne had been there more than once, and Daisy said that it would be a shame if she did not get to go out to it (on the lake). Randolph was not interested in going, she said, and Winterbourne said that it would please him to go to the castle with her. Realizing he had been bold, as he would not have been in Geneva, but seeing also that Daisy did not look offended at all, still Winterbourne added that he would like to go with her in the company of her mother. His concern seemed to be misplaced because Daisy said her mother probably would not go and the Eugenio, their courier (guide), could look after Randolph so that she and Winterbourne could go together.

> Comment

This is an example of the kind of openness and innocence that causes Daisy so much trouble later. One must understand that Daisy does not at all know the **conventions** of Europe. In the present time, the reader, especially in America, cannot see the gravity or importance of such unconventional behavior. It means, therefore, that one must not apply our contemporary standards to a society of the 1870s in Europe. Winterbourne is sincerely surprised when a young girl proposes to go to a shrine with him unescorted. Of course, the more literal European interpretation will emerge in the approaching character, Eugenio.

Winterbourne felt like kissing the hand of the young girl for her proposal, but at that moment Eugenio, a handsome man, approached, and Daisy greeted him in a very friendly manner. Eugenio announced luncheon. Daisy told him that she was going to the castle. Eugenio showed enough surprise that even Daisy sensed something and reacted by teasing Winterbourne that he was not going to back out, was he? Daisy was blushing. But she went on and asked Winterbourne if he really were an American. Winterbourne told her that he would introduce her to a person who would soon tell her all about him. Daisy turned and left with Eugenio, who had been standing there offensively.

Winterbourne did not realize how much he had actually promised in telling Daisy that he would introduce her to his aunt, Mrs. Costello. When he asked his aunt if she had seen the Americans, she said she had, with their courier, and had stayed out of their way. Mrs. Costello was a widow with a fortune. Two of her sons were married and lived in New York. A third son was in Europe but never seemed to be in the same city as his mother. Winterbourne, her nephew, was attentive to her, and she took it upon herself to inform him of the secrets of society. He could guess that the Millers were very low on her scale. When he asked if she approved of them, she said, "They are the sort of Americans that one does one's duty by not-not accepting." To her, Daisy was common and was intimate with her courier. Probably, Mrs. Costello thought, Daisy thought her courier some kind of Count. Winterbourne tried to explain that he thought the girl charming and wanted to introduce her to his aunt. She of course had great reservations about American girls, but when she heard that her nephew intended to visit the castle with Daisy on such short acquaintance, she refused to be introduced to her. As she put it, "I am an old woman, but I am not too old -thank Heaven - to be shocked!" Winterbourne pleaded that he thought all American girls acted like Daisy, but Mrs. Costello heard none of that.

Comment

The reader can see that Mrs. Costello lives in her own self-centered world. She is aware of class distinctions and she does not approve of the behavior of Daisy because the unwritten, but important laws do not prescribe her behavior. Mrs. Costello is the voice of **convention** and formality. She considers herself better than the Millers and warns her nephew to stay away from the girl. It is this rigid interpretation of behavior that has such dire consequences in the story.

Winterbourne did not know how he was going to tell Daisy about his aunt's refusal to see her, but when he saw Daisy that evening, he saw that she was concerned with other things. At first they talked about he brother, but later Daisy said that she had not seen the lady that Winterbourne wanted to introduce to her. She knew it was his aunt and knew about her headaches every two days. She said that she would like very much to meet her. Winterbourne said that his aunt's headaches would interfere. Finally, Daisy said to him that he need not be afraid to tell her the truth. Winterbourne tried to make excuses, but Daisy continued, "Why should she want to know me?" A few moments later, she exclaimed, "Gracious! She is exclusive."

Comment

Since the story is told from the point of view of Winterbourne, there is no direct evidence of how Daisy feels about this first social rejection. Certainly, there is a tone of innocent and impressed awe in her "exclusive," but one wonders if she is really hurt, as Winterbourne, himself puzzled, does. Probably, she is hurt, as her behavior in the second part of the story would indicate.

Before Winterbourne, prepared as he was to denounce his aunt in conversation, could say anything, Daisy exclaimed in quite another tone that her mother was coming. Winterbourne thought he should go away because the mother would not approve, but Daisy insisted that he stay. Daisy introduced him to Mrs. Miller, who had not been successful in getting Randolph to bed. Winterbourne agreed with his aunt that Mrs. Miller was common, but he felt that she had a delicate grace. At first they discussed Randolph and his late hours, but then Daisy told her mother that this was the man she was going to the castle with. Winterbourne expected that the mother would strongly disapprove, but quite to the contrary, she continued talking normally. Eventually, she agreed that Daisy should go but she herself was not interested.

Comment

The ineffectual mother who cannot handle her son and cannot understand the involvements of her daughter is in her own way a grown-up version of the innocence of her daughter. She too is an American portrait.

To Winterbourne's great surprise, Daisy suddenly asked him if he were not going to take her out to the castle that evening in a boat. Even Mrs. Miller was surprised at this and thought Daisy would prefer to stay indoors. But Daisy insisted she wanted to go no matter how late in the evening it was, and Winterbourne thought it would be a new sensation to guide a skiff through the summer starlight. Before they could go, however, Mrs. Miller told them they should find out what time it was. At that point the voice of Eugenio, with its foreign accent, informed them that it was eleven o'clock. Eugenio told Daisy that he did not think she should go out at that hour. Daisy responded to Eugenio that nothing she did was proper. Then, when Eugenio found that Daisy intended to go to the castle with Winterbourne and not her mother, he said solemnly, "As mademoiselle pleases!" Daisy turned to Winterbourne; he still wanted to go. But the girl changed and took leave from the gentleman. "I hope you are disappointed, or disgusted, or something!" she said. Winterbourne replied that he was puzzled.

Comment

These impulsive changes of Daisy puzzle Winterbourne. As the story progresses, one begins to realize that the figure of Europeanized Winterbourne is actually struggling to understand Daisy, but the point that he constantly cannot apprehend is her sudden bursts of spontaneity. His sedate, settled, orthodox responses, conditioned by the training of his aunt, are not preparation enough for him.

Two days later, Winterbourne met Daisy at the hotel and they went to the Castle of Chillon by steamboat because Daisy preferred that way. Daisy was elegantly dressed. Winterbourne was somewhat surprised by the casual and animated discussion of Daisy, for to him the trip was a very special excursion, but he saw that it was not that at all to her. He at first had some fears about the way she would behave, but soon he realized that he was charmed by her talk, by her behavior, and her open nature. Daisy chided him about his grave face, but he told her that he had never been so pleased in his life.

At the castle Daisy seemed little interested in the stories of antiquities that Winterbourne told her about the place; in the most curious places, she would suddenly ask him questions about himself, his family, his tastes, for example. About herself, she told all. Then she told him that he should accompany them in order to act as tutor for Randolph, but Winterbourne said he had other matters and would be leaving for Geneva the very next day. For the next ten minutes, Daisy called him horrid and asked about the "charmer" back in Geneva who would not give him more than three days away at a time. Winterbourne was stunned, especially since he always denied that there was a woman in Geneva for him. Finally, Winterbourne realized that Daisy was teasing him and would stop as soon as he promised to come down to Rome in the winter. Winterbourne said that would be an easy promise because his aunt had taken a place in Rome and had already asked him to visit her. Daisy told him that she was not interested in his coming to see his aunt, she wanted him to come for her.

Comment

It is these pleas that Winterbourne does not understand. Like so many American girls in the American novel, Daisy is trying to say something, but it is not being understood.

That evening Winterbourne told Mrs. Costello that he had spent the afternoon at Chillon with Daisy Miller. When she found that they had gone alone, Mrs. Costello responded, "And that is the young person whom you wanted me to know!"

Comment

The last statement in the first part of the story is a harsh prelude to the second part.

DAISY MILLER

TEXTUAL ANALYSIS

PART II

....

Towards the end of January Winterbourne went from Geneva to Rome. He had letters from his aunt and she had reported that the Millers, with their courier, had arrived and Daisy had taken up with some "third-rate Italians." When Winterbourne saw his aunt, he told her that he would see the Millers. His aunt told him that Daisy was going out alone with foreigners and that she was arriving at parties with a gentleman "with a good deal of manner and a wonderful moustache." The mother obviously was not accompanying the daughter. Winterbourne insisted that they were only ignorant and innocent, but Mrs. Costello responded when her nephew said he knew that they were not bad. She said they were "hopelessly vulgar."

Comment

Mrs. Costello makes an interesting point that characterizes her way of seeing things. She is not concerned with whether "vulgar" and "bad" are the same, she says. So far as she is concerned, the Millers are bad enough to dislike. The reader must remember that Mrs. Costello belongs to a society that measures things and people by manners. These manners become almost a moral problem to her kind. The bad manners of the Millers strike Mrs. Costello as unbearable in a much more significant way than we can imagine. To her they are not innocent people, but bad people.

The news that Daisy was surrounded by half-a-dozen moustaches disappointed Winterbourne because he thought the girl would be anxiously awaiting him. He decided to hold off his visit to Daisy for a while and to visit some other friends. He was at one lady's house no more than ten minutes when a servant announced Mrs. Miller. Winterbourne saw Randolph come in followed by Daisy and her mother. Daisy exchanged greetings with her hostess, Mrs. Walker, and was surprised to see Winterbourne. She told him that she had thought that he would visit her. Randolph told Winterbourne that their apartment was bigger than the one they were in and also that his mother was suffering from dyspepsia. Instead of being embarrassed, Mrs. Miller discussed her ailment and bemoaned the fact that she did not have her American doctor there. They were disappointed in Rome, she said. Daisy, on the other hand, was enjoying Rome because she knew the society and was going around everywhere.

Comment

The innocence of Mrs. Miller does certainly strike the reader almost as being ignorant. Her daughter's behavior is many times defiant, as the reader soon sees, but Mrs. Miller remains almost entirely a type of blank innocence. There is perhaps some ironic humor in her not understanding that her daughter's running around with the Italians is frowned upon by the other people.

At this point Daisy teased Winterbourne that she was complaining about him to Mrs. Walker. She complained that Winterbourne had treated them badly at Vevey by leaving. Mrs. Walker tried to support Winterbourne, but Daisy continued talking and told Mrs. Walker that she was accepting her invitation to her party. She also asked for permission to bring a friend, a Mr. Giovanelli. Mrs. Walker gave her assent, and Daisy explained that Giovanelli was an Italian, "the handsomest man in the world-except Mr. Winterbourne."

Comment

Again, Henry James gives many indications of Daisy's desperate desires to be accepted. Her teasing and confusing of Winterbourne probably cover her ignorance and nothing more. She does not know how to express herself. Her relation with Giovanelli is something else. The reader should not think that Daisy is playing off one man against the other. True to the character that the author has presented to this point, Daisy would be too innocent to think in those terms.

At this point Mrs. Miller said that they would have to return to their hotel, but Daisy said she was going for a walk on the Pincio. Mrs. Walker was visibly upset that Daisy intended to walk alone in the streets. Daisy said that she would not be alone because she was going to meet an Italian. Mrs. Walker found this even less acceptable. Daisy then proposed that, if it was improper, then perhaps Winterbourne could escort her to her rendezvous.

They left the apartment. Outside Daisy told Eugenio that she was going for a walk. When Winterbourne realized the peculiar circumstance, he was at once annoyed and gratified to be with Daisy as they walked. Daisy again asked him why he had not visited her. She talked rapidly about their quarters in Rome in her usual manner. Daisy spotted Giovanelli. Winterbourne noticed him: "he had a handsome face, an artfully poised hat. A glass in one eye and a nosegay in his buttonhole." Winterbourne did not approve and told Daisy that he intended to stay with her. Daisy looked right at her companion; clearly she said she did not like the way he said that, it was too imperious. She said that she had never allowed a gentleman to dictate to her or interfere with anything she did. Winterbourne told her that she should sometimes listen to the right man. When Daisy asked him if Giovanelli were that right gentleman, Winterbourne looked at the now close, smiling fellow and said no.

Comment

Daisy's independent statement that she allows no man to dictate to her is an important insight into her free and independent nature.

Daisy introduced the men to each other by name, and the three began walking together. Winterbourne did not like the Italian: he was not a gentleman, thought Winterbourne, but a music-master or a third-rate artist. Winterbourne concluded, "Nevertheless, a nice girl ought to know!" He was disturbed over the behavior of Daisy, and he found it hard to understand. He knew there was a want of delicacy, and her behavior was a combination of innocence and audacity.

They continued walking for a quarter of an hour. Then Winterbourne saw Mrs. Walker beckoning to him from a vehicle. Winterbourne hastened to obey and went over to the lady, who immediately said that Daisy's behavior was "dreadful." She felt it was a pity to allow the girl to ruin herself. Winterbourne insisted that she was very innocent, but Mrs. Walker asked him to think of the imbecility of the mother also. At the moment, the lady told Winterbourne to get Daisy into her carriage to preserve her honor. Winterbourne went to Daisy and asked her to speak to Mrs. Walker. Daisy came over and commented on the lady's carriage, but Mrs. Walker wasted no time and told her to get in. Daisy replied that she found her walk enchanting. Mrs. Walker replied, "It may be enchanting, dear child, but it is not the custom here." Daisy replied that it ought to be then. Mrs. Walker began to lose her patience, but Daisy did not want to get into the carriage. Mrs. Walker then asked her if she preferred to be considered "a reckless girl." Daisy was surprised. She turned and asked Winterbourne if she should get into the carriage to save her reputation. Winterbourne colored, but he had to tell her the truth only as he knew it. He told her to get in the carriage. Daisy laughed violently. She refused and turned away with Giovanelli. Mrs. Walker had tears in her eyes as she commanded Winterbourne into her carriage. Winterbourne hesitated a moment, but then said farewell to Daisy and Giovanelli.

Comment

This incident makes the contrast of the American and the European very distinct, perhaps too much so. Daisy defies Mrs. Walker because she is independent and must act as she knows how. She does not know how else to react when she is commanded. The reader finds at the end of the story that she has nothing to hide. Again, it is the innocence of Daisy that causes her to act. Winterbourne, on the other hand, although he believe that Daisy is innocent, still realizes the importance of what others believe. He does not want her to be in public with the Italian, he recommends that she get in the carriage, and he responds to the command of Mrs. Walker.

In the carriage, Winterbourne tried to support Daisy, but Mrs. Walker was insistent. She claimed that Daisy was out late in the evenings with the Italians and entertained them at home while the mother was out. He tried to explain that probably Daisy's brother was there, but Mrs. Walker could only guess at what the little boy was seeing. The servants were talking about her, said the lady. Winterbourne tried to defend Daisy: "The poor girl's only fault is that she is very uncultivated." Mrs. Walker asked the young man not to see Daisy anymore and not participate in the scandal. Winterbourne said he liked the girl very much and could not give her up. Mrs. Walker had said her piece so Winterbourne left the carriage. He saw Daisy and the Italian, but instead of walking towards them, he headed towards his aunt's house, Mrs. Costello's.

Winterbourne called at the Miller's twice but did not find them in. The third day was the day of Mrs. Walker's party. Mrs. Walker was one of the American ladies who made a point of studying European manners. Daisy was not there when Winterbourne arrived, but he saw Mrs. Miller talking to the hostess. He went over and found that they were talking about Daisy's coming with Giovanelli later. Mrs. Walker was quite upset at the talk of Mrs. Miller, and she said that she would not talk to Daisy when she arrived.

Daisy finally did come and walked right over to Mrs. Walker and told her that she was preparing Giovanelli so he could sing that evening. Daisy then asked if there was anyone she knew at the party. Mrs. Miller replied, "I think everyone knows you!" Giovanelli did sing later, but no one knew who asked him. Daisy spoke to Winterbourne about the incident with Mrs. Walker. Obviously, she did not see anything wrong with walking with Giovanelli. Winterbourne told her that she would be thought a flirt and he wished that she would flirt with him only. Daisy replied that he was "too stiff." Winterbourne asked her to stop flirting with Giovanelli. He told her that her behavior was not the custom there: "Flirting is a purely American custom; it doesn't exist here." He told her Giovanelli meant something quite different from innocent flirting. Daisy simply said that the two of them were friends and that Giovanelli never said such disagreeable things to her. Giovanelli then came to her side and asked her if she wanted some tea. Daisy teased Winterbourne and said that he never offered her tea. "I have offered you advice," Winterbourne said. Daisy cried, "I prefer weak tea!" and went off.

When Daisy was leaving that evening, Mrs. Walker carried out her vow. As Daisy came to say good night, Mrs. Walker turned her back on the girl. Winterbourne saw Daisy turn pale and look towards her mother. Mrs. Miller, typically, was unaware of anything, and said good night to Mrs. Walker. Winterbourne saw that Daisy was shocked. He went to Mrs. Walker and said to her, "That was very cruel." Mrs. Walker simply replied that Daisy would never enter her house again.

Comment

It is with this cruel rejection of Daisy by Mrs. Walker that the serious and complicated world of social behavior takes on a much greater significance than Daisy has imagined. Here the reader realizes that Daisy's defiance, her independence, her honest belief that she can do as she pleases and still participate in the society that she wants to be a part of-all these are not possible, for in order to be a part of that society, Daisy must live according to the rules of it. Daisy's shocked face, her grave face, shows that for the first time she has realized that this society could deeply hurt her. In our contemporary terms, we would assume that social rejection is not so important, but that is probably not a valid argument. Daisy is an archetype of the newly arrived young person with a different and limited background who believes that by being an individual and maintaining an individual code she can preserve her identity and still become part of a society that she wants to belong to. This rejection by Mrs. Walker proves quite the opposite is true. Just as Winterbourne has sacrificed all identity - and is therefore accepted - so the demand is that Daisy sacrifice herself. That is exactly what *Daisy Miller* is about: can Daisy, in her innocence, in her independence, also concede to the standards of a different society?

Since Winterbourne knew that he could not see Daisy at Mrs. Walker's, he started to go to the Millers' hotel. The women were usually out, but when Daisy was in, Giovanelli was always there. Winterbourne thought that Daisy could not surprise him any longer: "the unexpected in her behavior was the only thing to expect." He was amazed that his arrival never seemed to bother her and that she would continue to talk away without interruption. Daisy paid, in his presence, all her attention to Giovanelli and seemed interested only in him.

One Sunday afternoon. Winterbourne saw Daisy and Giovanelli at St. Peter's. Mrs. Costello, with whom he was there, looked at Daisy and said to her nephew, "That's what makes you so pensive these days, eh?" She told him that she had heard from several people that there was intrigue in the relationship between Daisy and Giovanelli. Winterbourne insisted that Daisy would not marry Giovanelli and had no such purpose. He had found out that the Italian was a respectable person, but not of the "first circles." He was a handsome man with no wealth. Winterbourne still thought that the Millers lacked culture, but he thought they were capable of acquiring it. Some friends of Mrs. Costello's arrived and they all discussed Daisy. Winterbourne felt sorry for her. One day, a tourist friend told Winterbourne that he had seen Daisy at a gallery with an Italian, and that caused him to rush to Mrs. Miller. That lady, however, simply told him that Daisy was out with Giovanelli and that the two were together so often that she had told Daisy that she looked as if she were engaged. Mrs. Miller said that she thought she would write to her husband although Daisy denied any such thing. Winterbourne decided that it would be utterly useless to try to put Mrs. Miller on guard.

Comment

Mrs. Miller is consistent in her innocence, and as such continues throughout the story as a basic contrast to the other people beside her daughter. She may be innocent, but the reader will find at the end of the tale that she has been the only one who was right in trusting that her daughter had maintained her virtue. The innocence of Mrs. Miller is such that it almost protects completely.

After this Daisy was never at home, and the society people were not inviting her to their homes. Winterbourne heard talk that her behavior was not typical of American girls. Daisy's innocence became for Winterbourne a "matter of fine-spun gallantry." One day he saw her at the ruins of the Palace of the Caesars. Daisy talked to him and Giovanelli acted properly. She assumed that he did not approve of her going around with the

Italian so much, but she was not aware of the way the "others" felt. Winterbourne said that they would snub her as had Mrs. Walker. Daisy said, "I shouldn't think you would let people be so unkind!" She said he could help by saying something. He told her that her mother thought she was engaged to Giovanelli, but Daisy denied that and told her friend not to believe it, as he said he did.

Comment

It is important to note Daisy's thoughts after the snub of Mrs. Walker. Many readers believe that Daisy plays off Giovanelli against Winterbourne. While it may be true that she is continuing her defiance, and is probably aware of it, it is wrong to think of her in this way, for Daisy is openly honest and clear in this conversation. That persistent honesty is very much in keeping with her plain innocence. Daisy is simply being herself. She wants very much to be accepted in the upper circles of society, but she must also be herself.

A week later, after dining at a restaurant, Winterbourne decided to walk into the Colosseum, a famous Roman landmark. He entered the vast area and walked toward the large cross in the center. On the base of it he saw a man and a woman sitting in the dark. Then he heard the voice of Daisy Miller, "Well, he looks at us as one of the old lions or tigers may have looked at the Christian martyrs!" At that point, Winterbourne suddenly decided that Daisy was a young lady that a gentleman need not respect. He was angry that he had ever cared about what she was doing and turned to leave. But Daisy called to him. He knew that she was sitting in the nest of malaria. Sharply, he asked her how long she had been there and reminded her of the Roman fever. Giovanelli said that he had told the girl the same thing.

Winterbourne told her she should go home, and Giovanelli immediately went after their carriage. Daisy asked him if he really believed that she was engaged, and Winterbourne replied that what he believed made no difference at all now. When Giovanelli came with a cab, Winterbourne admonished her to take her pills, but Daisy called back that she did not care if she got Roman fever.

Winterbourne told no one about Daisy's being in the Colosseum at midnight, but within two days the little American circle was talking about it. A day or two later, Winterbourne heard that Daisy was very ill. Winterbourne found Mrs. Miller a good and patient nurse. The mother told him that Daisy was delirious, but that she had sent word to him that she was never engaged to Giovanelli. A week later Daisy died. She was buried in a small Protestant cemetery. At the funeral, Winterbourne stood near Giovanelli, who at last told Winterbourne that Daisy was the most beautiful young lady he knew, "and she was the most innocent." Winterbourne was surprised at this, but the Italian repeated it emphatically. Then Giovanelli said that Daisy never would have married him. Winterbourne was surprised.

He left Rome immediately, but the following summer he again met his aunt. During the course of a conversation, he mentioned Daisy and said that he felt he had done her an injustice. The aunt asked him how, and he explained that on her death bed Daisy had sent him a message that he now understood but did not then. "She would have appreciated one's esteem," he said. The aunt wanted to know if that was a nice way of saying that if he were to have liked her, she would have responded. Winterbourne knew that what his aunt had said the previous summer - that he would make a mistake because he had been living in Europe too long - had come true. Winterbourne returned to Geneva and people say that he was "studying" hard there.

Comment

These last few pages hold much of the story. It is only at the end that Winterbourne realizes that Daisy had remained innocent to the very end. He also realizes that the girl had wanted desperately to be accepted. Because he had lived in Europe so long, he was not able to understand that. He interpreted Daisy as all the other Europeanized Americans. He had failed to realize that she had remained an honest girl and had suffered because of her individual and open nature.

DAISY MILLER

CHARACTER ANALYSES

DAISY MILLER

This figure that was once considered "an outrage on American girlhood" represents one of the highest accomplishments in American fiction. Daisy Miller has been considered the exact stereotype of the newly emerging American girl of the nineteenth century. She has been considered the embodiment of the independent western hero in female dress. She has been considered typically American because of her desperate efforts to be accepted by a higher society than the one she comes from. Some have considered her an example of freedom triumphant. Some have considered her bad. And at least one man has called her the "Good Bad Girl" that all American girls really are down deep.

The aspects of her character that are revealed in Henry James's story are fairly clear. It is the emphasis that is important. From the very beginning of the story, when the reader hears her scolding her brother, he realizes that Daisy is an unaffected, open, and honest young girl. She is very direct in her conversations with Winterbourne, the reader's analyst. Sometimes she is direct almost to a fault as when she wants impulsively to row out to the castle in the night. The important point is Daisy has no past to cover up. She is fresh and new. There is nothing devious about her.

Her overriding quality, moreover, is her innocence. All critics comment on that aspect of Daisy. To her, all things are new because she does not have the experience of the old world. Her innocence is such that she does not bother to interpret the laws of the society that she wants to enter. Daisy, however, can be defiant when she feels that her freedom is being interfered with, and it is with her defiance that Daisy shows that the old society is limited and narrow. This defiance of custom, of form and **convention**, and superstition, reveals perhaps deeper roots in her character. At the end of the story one realizes that Daisy did after all want to be accepted by the very people who were rejecting her. One can see that her actions have been the frustrated efforts of an immature and innocent girl to let the world know that she wants to join it. In other words, Daisy ultimately fails and pays with her life because she did not understand the society that did not understand her.

FREDERICK WINTERBOURNE

The central consciousness of the story is quite a different character from the heroine. Winterbourne has lived in Europe so long that he has forgotten completely how to behave with Americans. When he arrives from Geneva, that seat of Calvinism, he must run to his aunt for advice. He senses that there is something special in Daisy, but he is puzzled by her. Unconsciously, he chooses as his aunt dictates, and towards the end of the story, it seems that his moralistic tone, his desire to make Daisy do what people say she should, wins out. He finally decides that Daisy is not decent. He does not at all realize that he has not made his decision for himself but has accepted a decision that the society his aunt belongs to has made. Winterbourne, then, is a failure in the novel, no matter how one views him. He fails because he does not understand the desperate needs of Daisy. He fails because he has a chance to accept another human being and he does not understand it. He fails because he returns to the seat of Puritanism in Geneva. He fails because he cannot live with his emotions. He rejects them as he does life.

MRS. MILLER

As a characterization, Mrs. Miller does not have depth. As a person, Mrs. Miller is innocent in a shallow level. She is blandly unaware of the drama that her daughter is caught in. She is an ineffectual mother. Slight traces of grace appear-as when one realizes that she competently nurses the ill Daisy-but the portrait that remains is one of the frustrated mother who cannot handle her children.

RANDOLPH MILLER

Randolph is so typically American that he seems somewhat embarrassingly accurate. He is away from America and he misses the candy. He wants to leave this "old Europe," as he calls it. He is bold and precocious, harsh, and unmannered, but he is a telling contrast already to the sterile ways of the people of the conventional European world. One marvels at his rebellious spirit, its enduring strength against the weakness of the mother, forever caught in trying to get him to bed. The only defect in Randolph's portrait is probably that it is tellingly complete in such a brief work.

MRS. COSTELLO

Winterbourne's aunt, too, is a typical and stylized portrait. She has been living in Europe long enough that she can now look from above and cast her cutting comments on the Millers with freedom. All her judgments are made on the basis of two things and no others: first, Mrs. Costello judges people by appearances. She is not interested in them as people, but as examples of behavior. She immediately does not like the Millers because of the way they are friendly with their courier. Second, Mrs. Costello makes all her decisions on the basis of conventions. She constantly reminds her attentive nephew of what one should do and ought do. She considers Daisy loose and immoral. She cannot understand or see humanity, for people are what the code of her society decides they are. Although Mrs. Costello seems to win, Daisy has made a telling mark in the dangerous game of manners.

MRS. WALKER

Mrs. Walker, too, is bound by appearances. She tries to harness the freedom of Daisy. She orders her into her carriage because she says that society dictates that it is not proper for an American girl to walk unescorted with an Italian. Mrs. Walker, like Mrs. Costello, cannot understand the individual. When she turns her back on Daisy at the party, she epitomizes the potential evil in the selfish and narrow world she lives in. It is a world that cannot tolerate a new and fresh spirit. It is a world that rejects the young and independent. Mrs. Walker is the opposite of the things that Daisy represents, and she shows what extremes can emerge from her own beliefs.

GIOVANELLI

The handsome, stereotyped Italian is Daisy's constant companion in Rome. All the other people think that they have become intimate, but at Daisy's funeral Giovanelli shows that he has understood the beautiful and innocent American girl. He is not the third-rate artist that Mrs. Costello thinks he is. He shows himself with dignity and concern, a brief, but human position in a story that lacks, precisely and tragically, that very position.

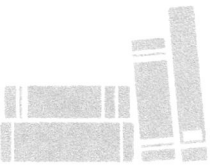

DAISY MILLER

CRITICAL COMMENTARY

HENRY JAMES'S "PREFACE" AND OTHER COMMENTS ON THE STORY

Henry James wrote a series of prefaces for a collected edition of his novels reissued by Charles Scribner's between 1907 and 1917. This collection is referred to as The New York Edition. In these prefaces he reviewed his problems in writing his works and many times pointed to special devices that he employed in working out his plots. In the preface to *Daisy Miller* James relates how in Rome a friend of his mentioned how a young American girl had "picked up" with a good-looking Italian and had gone along all innocently until she experienced a social check. James does not recall what the check was that he heard in 1877, but he recalls that that was the "germ" of his story. James goes on to explain that he submitted the story to a Philadelphia publisher and received it back from him with no comment. He found out later that the man had refused to publish it because the story would have passed as "an outrage on American girlhood." James explains that his sub-title, "A Study," was meant more for the reader than for the character, Daisy. He remembers once being in Venice with a female friend. The two of them observed two young children freely playing. His hostess commented that those were the real Daisy Millers and not the figure that James had distorted in his story. James's answer was that his heroine was of course "pure poetry," meaning that he had invented a fictional character.

In a letter written about 1880 to a Mrs. Linton, a minor English novelist, James included an explanation of his story. Among other things, there is a special emphasis he makes on how he intended Daisy to be understood. He says that the whole point of the story is the tragedy of an unsuspecting creature who is ultimately sacrificed to a "social rumpus" that she never understood. He continues that he added to the effect by having the mother not understand the whole thing.

CHRISTOF WEGELIN ON THE IMAGE OF EUROPE IN HENRY JAMES

The author sees this story as the classic example of the troubles the American girl has in Europe when she is confronted by the Europeanized Americans. These Americans want to advertise their conversion; they are social snobs, they want to show how fully aware they are of Daisy's socially unacceptable behavior before the Europeans, whom they imitate. Winterbourne, the point of view through whom Daisy is seen, is not a snob, but he has lived in Europe so long that he misjudges the American girl. James's **theme** is the "American snobbishness abroad" and the tragedy is the "death of individual responsibility at the hands of convention." But the story is not a tragedy, says the author; it is a comedy. Daisy is after all somewhat foolish.

TRISTRAM P. COFFIN ON DAISY MILLER AS A WESTERN HERO

Coffin says Daisy Miller is a western hero "with a parasol and a bank account." James gave her the personality traits that distinguish the western hero. She is not complex. She is open. Like the typical western hero, Daisy is happy to rely on herself and no one else. That is why she befriends the fortune hunter Giovanelli in defiance of everybody. There are differences from the usual western story. Usually, the western hero converts the society that he fights against, but James, the realistic writer, brings about the ending with tragedy.

LESLIE FIEDLER

In *Love and Death in the American Novel*, Fiedler asks why a figure such as Daisy Miller, with her unspeakable little brother, her shocked American admirer, and her affair with an Italian, shocked American womanhood when it first appeared in the nineteenth century. It is the manner of Daisy, not her morals, that so offended the people who read the work. What was so difficult to understand was how such a pure figure could be one who violates respectability so much. According to Fiedler, James emphasizes over and over again the innocence of Daisy. What the European fails to realize about American girls is that they are innocent by definition. They are innocent not by what they say or do, but by definition only. They are always "Good Bad Girls." No matter what her outward appearance, no matter how she behaves, according to the American definition, beneath it all, one finds that the American girl is always Good. Therefore, the Good Bad Girl.

THE VIEW OF F. W. DUPEE

Dupee says that *Daisy Miller* is a study of comparative manners and, because of the point of view of Winterbourne, a story of appearance and reality. From Winterbourne's way of seeing things, the reader has his doubts about the innocence of Daisy. He is uncertain about Daisy's behavior, but because of her death one finally ends up admiring her because she has died young and pretty. If one reads the story in this way, then the portrait of Daisy is purely a triumph, a triumph of radical innocence over the "evilmindedness of the old world." Then the question arises if she is innocent in the technical sense only. Even Winterbourne decides that she is bad after she runs around in defiance of custom. The Americans in Rome expect her to do as the Romans do, and she fails the test. To them, therefore, she is bad. They are wrong, and Winterbourne is wrong because he has lived too long in Europe.

But the story, looked at closely, reveals certain ironies. Daisy's death in the Colosseum is not noble, because she rejects the Roman superstition that one can die by being in the place at night and finds that the old superstition is true. Daisy laughs at these traditions, but she suffers because she has no traditions. Daisy is actually imprudent and "somewhat callow", even her manners are sometimes bad. She is a girl who does what she likes, but she is not able to express her love for Winterbourne, which is the cause for much of her behavior. Finally, Daisy lives in a vacuum that exists because of her wealth and her lack of real commitments. The story of Daisy is not a "tribute to the American girl."

JAMES W. GARGANO

According to Gargano, critics have been wrong in emphasizing the story of Daisy. They have failed to realize that Winterbourne is the center of the novel. From Winterbourne's first view of Vevey, one can see that the story is the initiation of a man who is leaving his world of fixed values. The critic says, "*Daisy Miller* is essentially the study of a young man's quest for innocence, a virtue from which his society has alienated itself." It is significant that Winterbourne meets Daisy in a garden in Vevey. He has come to Vevey because the atmosphere is not so rigid there as it is in Geneva. Winterbourne constantly misreads Daisy's actions because innocence is the very thing that is missing in the city from which he has come. Winterbourne's initiation begins in a comic manner when he decided to speak to Daisy, knowing full well that he would not do so in Geneva. He is confused by her innocence, so he runs to his aunt, Mrs. Costello. Despite what she says, he holds to his resolve of going to the Castle with the girl. Winterbourne only partially understands the freedom of Daisy, and after the trip, he makes a symbolic return to Geneva.

The Roman part of the story destroys Winterbourne's weak love of innocence in Daisy. He tries to defend Daisy, but he realizes that he has lived too long in Geneva. After the rejection of Daisy by Mrs. Walker, even Winterbourne no longer understands the innocence of the girl. Winterbourne's quest ends in a Puritan repudiation of innocence. Now he begins to see the evil nature in the girl. His last conversation proves that. He is convinced of that nature when she dies. After the funeral he broods over the judgment he has made of the girl, but at the end retreats of Geneva again and his quest has only proved his inadequacy.

Note: For the exact bibliographic data on these works discussed above and for many more studies of this work, the reader should consult the work edited by William T. Stafford in the Selected Bibliography.

DAISY MILLER

ESSAY QUESTIONS AND ANSWERS

Question: Discuss point of view in the narration of *Daisy Miller*. Emphasize particularly its significance in understanding certain aspects of character.

Answer: Henry James's story seems at first glance to be an objective story about the heroine, Daisy Miller. She seems to be viewed clearly and definitely, with very clear lines, so that the reader would think that he was reading a third person narrative with an omniscient narrator (that is to say, the author of the work acting as the narrator). One realizes shortly, however, that the picture of Daisy is not so objective as it would first appear. An obvious example is the point when Daisy realizes in the first part of the story that Winterbourne is not going to introduce her to his aunt, Mrs. Costello, as he had earlier promised he would. Daisy seems very casual about this at first, but then the reader realizes that she has gone to the trouble of finding out about Mrs. Costello, knowing the facts about her, and although she seems nonchalant, there is a hint that the girl would like to meet such a lady. Daisy says with almost open-eyed childishness, "Gracious, she is exclusive."

At the end of the story, the reader realizes that Daisy wanted very much to be accepted, and that realization causes one to reflect that internally Daisy might have been deeply concerned in the earlier scene. There seems to be, therefore, a difference between appearance and reality.

The basis for that difference is a complicated matter, and that brings one to the real aspect of point of view in the story. Daisy Miller, one notices, is seen only through the eyes of Winterbourne. She appears on one level only as she appears to Winterbourne. For example, when Winterbourne first arrives in Rome, he hears from Mrs. Costello that Daisy is moving in a circle of "mustached" Italians. The reader does not see that in the story. He must simply accept the fact, as Winterbourne does. This brings the reader to the next level of what James is able to accomplish with his selective point of view. Because Winterbourne is an individual - that is to say, has an individual character in the story - he interprets things in a social way. Of course, the reader knows that he relies on the opinions of his aunt and her type, but Winterbourne shows the reader what his real reaction is to the statements of his aunt when he decides to visit Daisy. In other words, Winterbourne is commenting on Daisy by what he does, not by any direct statement that he makes.

Therefore, point of view is important. It is a way of telling the story through one of the characters involved and it is a way of interpreting characters in the work. The reader sees Daisy through the view of Winterbourne, who himself constantly interprets. By choice, James is able to add much greater dimension.

Question: Many people have taken Henry James's subtitle, "A Study," quite literally. They assume that Daisy is a type. Discuss this matter.

Answer: When *Daisy Miller* first appeared, it was considered "an outrage on American girlhood." Allegedly, the character of Daisy was intended to be an example of American girlhood and the way that type would behave in Europe. Certain aspects of Daisy seem to bear out this interpretation. She is newly rich, she has little awareness of responsibility, she is quite independent, she is free, she is sometimes defiant, she is honest and innocent. To a certain degree, even James thought of the American character in these terms. On the other hand, there seem to be quite some other matters in this "study" that James wrote. Daisy also has some individual characteristics that are not exclusively American but are quite personal. For example, the reader realizes that Daisy has felt deeply the rejections of Mrs. Walker and her group. We find that Daisy is independent, but she is so much so that her behavior has deeper roots than an expression limited by type. Daisy seems defiant, even flippant. As one looks at any of these characteristics, he realizes a personal figure of a young girl, any young immature girl, is emerging. Daisy is a living person, not just a type. She feels things deeply, and she tries in her own way to express herself. Because she does not have the conventions to do so, one cannot find fault with her. Perhaps what is so successful in the character of Daisy is the fact that there have been so many imitations of her in later works.

When Henry James once was criticized because his typical American was not typical at all, he responded by saying to his critic that the major point was of course that his character was "poetry."

Question: Discuss the characters of Mrs. Costello and Mrs. Walker.

Answer: These are the two women who give Daisy her deepest rebuffs. In the first part of the story, Mrs. Costello refuses to be introduced to Daisy and her family. In the second part, Mrs. Walker, at her party, turns her back on Daisy when she approaches to say good evening. Why both of these women act as they do is very important in the story.

One can begin with Mrs. Walker, the expatriate American now living in Rome. When Mrs. Walker hears that Daisy is to walk alone on a Roman street, she is horrified. She tries to explain that one does not act that way because it simply is not the custom. Then, in an important scene, Mrs. Walker orders Daisy to get into her carriage to preserve her honor. Daisy refuses, and Mrs. Walker is indignant because Daisy's behavior is unacceptable. When at the party, Daisy arrives late with an Italian, makes him sing, and behaves as she pleases, Mrs. Walker feels that Daisy has violated the code of behavior as Americans in Europe understand it. Daisy is an affront, a danger, to her way of life, so Mrs. Walker in order to preserve that way of life rejects and ignores Daisy. Of course, it is a telling blow because Mrs. Walker does not realize that Daisy wants desperately to be accepted by Mrs. Walker's society. It is a matter of innocence that strikes one as gross ignorance.

Mrs. Costello also rejects Daisy, but hers may be a more pernicious and more dangerous act than that of Mrs. Walker. Mrs. Costello never meets with Daisy, but when her nephew mentions the Millers the first time, she has already observed them and has already made her decision about them. She does not like the way they behave with their courier. Quite definitely, condescendingly, she tells her nephew that the Millers are the kind of people that cause one to do his duty by ignoring. Mrs. Costello does just that. However, it is only on the surface that she ignores them. Always she knows what the Millers are doing, and always she recommends that her nephew, who is struggling to find a way to understand them, stay away from them. Mrs.

Costello, therefore, goes a step beyond Mrs. Walker in rejecting Daisy. She cannot stand her because of what she represents and she is incapable of understanding that the Americans are innocent. To her, their innocence is reprehensible.

One realizes at the end of the story that Mrs. Costello has not been touched by the tragedy of Daisy. Her decisions with her nephew have won out. It is an ending that is sterile because it admits of no new people, new ideas, or fresh behavior.

4. Discuss the ending of the story.

Answer: Actually, the ending of *Daisy Miller* begins in the dark of the famous Colosseum. When Winterbourne sees Daisy there, in defiance of Roman superstition and in defiance of the **conventions** of society, he decides that she is not a girl worth worrying over. It is a deflation for Winterbourne: he thinks he now knows that Daisy is a bad girl. Then suddenly, too suddenly, Daisy dies of malaria, but it is at her funeral that the next stage of the ending becomes clear. Winterbourne hears from the good-looking Italian, Giovanelli, that Daisy would never have married him. Directly, clearly, Giovanelli insists that Daisy was a good girl and a very innocent one. The reader can sense that Winterbourne is shaken by this statement. He realizes that he may have been too harsh. The true ending of the story comes during the next summer. By this time, Winterbourne is ready to admit he has been wrong in his interpretation of Daisy. He realized too late that the young girl was very much concerned with being accepted. It is the first indication that Daisy has finally made her mark. But it is Mrs. Costello who gets the last word and the show of triumph. She states that the girl had a curious way of showing that she wanted acceptance. On that, Winterbourne returns to Geneva. The world of the society he knows has not changed at all, although he may have.

SELECTED BIBLIOGRAPHY AND GUIDE TO RESEARCH

There are no really significant separate studies of *Washington Square*, other than perhaps the "Preface" to the Dell Laurel Edition by R. P. Blackmur previously cited. The key to further research on *Washington Square*, in the opinion of the present author, lies in the study of the relation of that work to the **theme** of vampirism, as discussed in the section on James's morality, above.

Oscar Cargill's *The Novels of Henry James* (New York: Macmillan, 1961), while rather neglecting a detailed account of *Washington Square* in favor of what are generally considered the more major novels of James, can provide a valuable overview of Jamesian fiction for the student.

Since there is so much that has been written on James, the student must have some principle of selection. This can be accommodated under the headings of Biography, Criticism, and Bibliography. Consultation of the following works, at a minimum, will at least insure that the student will read a good selection of the better and more useful articles and books bearing on James in general and on the particular works of James.

BIOGRAPHY

The best place to begin on the biography of Henry James is his own works: *A Small Boy and Others*, 1913; *Notes of a Son and Brother*, 1914; and *The Middle Years*, 1917. These three volumes, which contain many important reflections by James on his family and personal life, are edited in one volume by F. W. Dupee, *Henry James's Autobiography*, 1956.

The outstanding biography of Henry James, and an outstanding biography in itself, is written by Leon Edel, who reconstructs the life of James from all possible sources, especially from his letters. The biography will be in four volumes when it is completed. At the present, three volumes have appeared: *Henry James: The Untried Years, 1843-1870*, 1953; *Henry James: The Conquest of London, 1870-1881*, and *Henry James: The Middle Years, 1882-1895*, both in 1962. The fourth volume, *The Master, 1895-1916*, is in preparation.

An excellent one-volume study of James with very sound criticism throughout and an excellent view of James's career is F. W. Dupee's *Henry James*, 1951.

Of importance in studying James fully are his letters: *Selected Letters of Henry James*, edited by Leon Edel, 1960.

CRITICISM

All James's students should begin with two edited works of James's own writings, for they contain extraordinary insight into the problems that he faced as a writer and a critic. James's methods of writing and making notes can best be seen in *The*

Notebooks of Henry James, edited by F. O. Matthiessen and Kenneth Murdock, 1947. James's "Prefaces" are collected in a separate volume by R. P. Blackmur, who supplies an excellent introduction with an analysis of the subjects of the prefaces and their general ideas. The volume is published as *The Art of the Novel*, 1959.

All the literary histories of American literature contain chapters on Henry James, and a beginning student will do well to begin with one of these. A long chapter by R. P. Blackmur on James in the *Literary History of the United States*, 1948, gives a complete view of James.

Of the separate volumes on James, a very useful one for the student is a collection of essays edited by F. W. Dupee, *The Question of Henry James*, 1945. There are discussions and essays by different critics on most of the problems in James study.

One early study, which was particularly critical of James's expatriation to Europe and questioned the whole idea of Europe because it was seen too idealistically by the later James, was Van Wyck Brooks's *The Pilgrimage of Henry James*, 1925.

A very detailed, though somewhat dated, and excellent analysis of the backgrounds and the significance of James' style is done by Joseph Warren Beach, *The Method of Henry James*, 1918.

A short and general view of the whole subject, very valuable to the beginning student, is Leon Edel's *Henry James*, 1960, *University of Minnesota Pamphlets on American Writers*.

BIBLIOGRAPHY

Almost all of the above works have useful bibliographies for the beginning student. These in turn will lead on to other studies on Henry James.

A good descriptive bibliography, that organizes the criticism of James in order for the student, is the one by Robert E. Spiller in *Eight American Authors: A Review of Research and Criticism*, edited by Floyd Stovall, 1956.

A much fuller bibliography is Leon Edel's and D. H. Laurence's *A Bibliography of Henry James*, 1958.

DAISY MILLER

The student will find an excellent text and the essays discussed in the Critical Commentary, plus many others, in William T. Stafford, editor, *James's* Daisy Miller*: The Story, The Play, The Critics*, 1963.

TURN OF THE SCREW

The best essays and the text of this work are collected in Gerald Willen's *A Casebook on Henry James's* The Turn of the Screw, 1960. The essays discussed in the Critical Commentary are in that volume.

www.ingramcontent.com/pod-product-compliance
Lightning Source LLC
LaVergne TN
LVHW011712060526
838200LV00051B/2882